# THE SMART GUIDE TO

# United States Visas

# BY SCOTT SYFERT AND MELISA BORIS

**The Smart Guide To United States Visas**

Published by

Smart Guide Publications, Inc.
2517 Deer Chase Drive
Norman, OK 73071
www.smartguidepublications.com

For information, address: Smart Guide Publications, Inc. 2517 Deer Creek Drive, Norman, OK 73071

SMART GUIDE and Design are registered trademarks licensed to Smart Guide Publications, Inc.

International Standard Book Number: 978-1-937636-00-5

Library of Congress Catalog Card Number: 2012932059
11 12 13 14 15   10 9 8 7 6 5 4 3 2 1

*Printed in the United States of America*

Cover design: Lorna Llewellyn
Copy Editor: Ruth Strother
Back cover design: Joel Friedlander, Eric Gelb, Deon Seifert
Back cover copy: Eric Gelb, Deon Seifert
Illustrations: Lorna Llewellyn
Production: Zoë Lonergan
Indexer: Cory Emberson
V.P./Business Manager: Cathy Barker

# TABLE OF CONTENTS

# INTRODUCTION

Traveling to another country is always exciting, whether you're traveling for business or for pleasure. The unknown possibilities of what you'll find once you step over the border are irresistible to many people. What will it be like? Will the people be friendly? Will the food be good?

Often hand in hand with excitement is anxiety. You may wonder if the culture will seem completely different or if you will fit in. Probably one of the biggest anxieties foreign nationals face when coming to the United Sates is whether they have all their papers in order. Will their visa be solid enough to allow them into the United States?

## Who Should Read This Book

Foreign nationals are not the only ones who should have an understanding of the visa system. Our post-9/11 world makes it increasingly important for anyone with any contact with the visa system, including employers, student advisors, and policy makers, to understand the immigration laws and procedures imposed by the U.S. government.

This book will help you whether you are the human resources director of a multinational company, a foreign student who would like to study at a U.S university, a U.S. citizen who would like to marry a foreign national, a law student interested in practicing immigration law, or a seasoned attorney searching for more detail about a particular visa category.

### What You Will Learn

After you have read this book, you will have a working knowledge of the fundamentals of U.S. visa law. We simplify complex concepts and explain critical terms that you need to know to avoid missteps either while in front of a U.S. immigration inspector, at an embassy abroad, or in a filing with a governmental agency. In short, this book gives anyone coming in contact with the U.S. visa system the basic tools for success. Think of this book as a map that helps you navigate the wilderness of the U.S. visa system efficiently, without fear, and without getting lost.

## Welcome to America!

Most people are introduced to U.S. visas the hard way.

Imagine you're a foreigner on your first visit to the United States. You have just completed a ten-hour flight. It is 5 a.m. You are tired, groggy, and uncertain. Maybe you don't speak English well—maybe you don't speak English at all. You have heard horror stories on TV or from your friends about strict new security measures in the United States: long lines, tough questions, fingerprinting, and so forth.

As you stand patiently in line waiting to go through immigration, you are, quite understandably, nervous. What if they don't let you in? What if you say the wrong thing? Will you end up in Gitmo?

After waiting with a hundred or so equally bedraggled foreign travelers, your number is called. You drag your carry-on luggage behind you and walk tentatively forward. Sitting behind a desk is a U.S. immigration inspector. He does not look particularly friendly. You hand him your passport. He slides it through a machine, looks at a computer, and then looks at you.

You are face-to-face with the U.S. government. What should you say? What should you do?

## *Say the Right Thing*

Put yourself in the shoes of the immigration inspector. Remember that he, too, is tired. He has interviewed travelers all day, some of whom were rude or even aggressive. His job is unrewarding, difficult, and stressful—after all, he is the last line of defense before a potential drug smuggler or terrorist is admitted into the country.

Now it's your turn. The inspector has roughly thirty seconds to look at you, check your name in a database, and decide whether or not you should be admitted to the United States. If he has any doubts about you or the purpose of your visit to the United States, he is well within his rights to detain you for additional interrogation, a process called secondary inspection or just secondary.

### Advice of Counsel

Be polite; rude behavior is not recommended. There is no quicker way to make your life difficult than by pissing off the inspector.

Equally important is to say the right thing. Of course, tell the truth—that goes without saying. Being caught in a prevarication, or lie, will get you into secondary for sure. Immigration lawyers have a common saying: the only mistake that you cannot correct is fraud. You can almost always fix your visa problems, provided you don't commit fraud. In short, don't lie. What you say should be both true, meaning the facts support it, and correct, meaning it won't set off any alarm bells or red flags with the government. Also important: know what not to say.

## Terminology

Imagine, for example, you are coming into the United States without a visa pursuant to what is called a visa waiver. In this case, you are not allowed to work while in the United States. If the inspector asks, "What is the purpose of your visit to the United States?" don't say, "I'm here to work."

### Advice of Counsel

Never miss an opportunity to shut up. You are required to truthfully answer the questions the government asks you. You are not required to expound at length or volunteer information, except in rare circumstances. Answer the questions you are asked truthfully and briefly; then keep your mouth shut.

But suppose the purpose of your trip is business—you will be engaged in a series of meetings with clients. Isn't this work?

Although the visa waiver rules do not allow work and employment while in the United States, visiting the United States to engage in business meetings, to speak with clients or potential clients, and so forth is allowed. This is an important distinction. So in this context the answer, "I'm here to work," is incorrect. The correct answer would be, "I'm here to meet with business colleagues on behalf of my employer, a large foreign company."

Note that both answers may be true, but the first answer may make it difficult for you to enter the United States, while the second answer will have you collecting your baggage in five minutes.

### Advice of Counsel

Immigration inspectors are schooled in the regulations, policies, and laws governing the admittance of U.S. citizens and foreigners to the United States. They go through police training, and most have an undergraduate degree. Inspectors know their stuff, so it's not a good idea to try to outwit them. Just be honest.

In short, a basic working knowledge of U.S. visa law may mean the difference between the inspector saying, "Welcome to the United States of America!" and "Come with me. I want to ask you some additional questions."

# Be in the Know

Knowledge is power. And nowhere is this truer than in navigating the uncertain and potentially dangerous waters of the U.S. visa system. It is a system that is complex and convoluted with bewildering terms. It is also a system where a mistake or a misstatement or even a paperwork error can be devastating. Understanding the lay of the land, the concepts, and the proper terminology can mean the difference between entering the United States and spending the night in a windowless government office at the airport—or worse.

## *Understanding Visa Lingo*

U.S. visa law is full of terms that are familiar to those who understand the system, such as government officials or immigration lawyers, but are baffling to those who do not. Of course, you cannot be expected to know or understand all of these terms, much less all the nuances of this area of law.

In addition, there are a handful of key forms that are designated by government acronyms. For example, most every applicant around the world must complete the DS-160 electronic form to apply for a visa (*DS* refers to the Department of State.) Similarly, most business visa applicants must receive an I-797 form, the approval notice, to apply for a visa in the first place.

As we go along, we will highlight these key terms and forms for you.

# Who's Who in the Visa World

We can't go much further without introducing the main governmental actors in the visa world. These are known by various acronyms. Until March 2003, much of U.S. visa and immigration policy was controlled by the Immigration and Naturalization Service (INS).

The INS no longer exists, although the term is sometimes still used because everyone knows what it stands for.

Following the 9/11 attacks, the Department of Homeland Security (DHS) became the controlling agency for all U.S. immigration matters. INS was renamed and reorganized, and its functions were divided into several agencies under the umbrella of the DHS: United States Citizenship and Immigration Services (USCIS), Customs and Border Protection (CBP), and Immigration and Customs Enforcement (ICE).

Together with the U.S. Department of State (DOS), these four federal agencies—DHS, USCIS, CBP, and ICE—control or regulate virtually all aspects of the U.S. visa world. The USCIS and DOS in particular have primary responsibility to adjudicate and issue U.S. visas.

# Our Game Plan

For this book, our game plan is to begin by discussing two key distinctions that are absolutely fundamental to understanding the U.S. visa system: immigrant vs. nonimmigrant and visa vs. status. Understanding these terms will give you a firm grounding in the basic concepts that underlie all U.S. visa law.

### Visa Vocab

An *immigrant* is a green card holder or applicant. A *nonimmigrant* is every other foreign national. This book deals exclusively with nonimmigrant visas (NIV).

A *visa* is simply the stamp in your passport; *status* is your legal situation while you are in the United States.

In part two we discuss the process of obtaining a visa. As you may have figured out by now, obtaining a visa is somewhat complicated and, depending upon the visa, may involve several different governmental agencies—particularly USCIS (which approves certain types of visas) and DOS (which actually issues visas).

In part three we discuss in detail the most common temporary, or nonimmigrant, visas such as visas for business visitors, executives, and aliens of extraordinary ability. In part four we cover the common and well-known NIV categories for students, trainees, nannies, and fiancés. In part five we address questions that NIV holders commonly have.

## *Finally…*

While this book is designed to be a comprehensive guide to U.S. nonimmigrant visas, it is not a comprehensive guide to all facets of U.S. immigration law. For example, this book does not offer thorough information about the lawful permanent resident (green card) process, nor does it address methods for becoming a U.S. citizen. This book also does not deal with specialized topics such as asylum or refugees. There is a plethora of information on these subjects available on the Internet or in specialized books. In many cases, the issues are sufficiently complex that you may wish to consider hiring a lawyer to handle them.

Finally, note that the U.S. immigration system is in a constant state of flux, now more than ever. It is important for those who must brave the system to obtain the knowledge they will need to avoid pitfalls and ultimately to succeed.

Whatever your purpose for reading this book, we hope to provide the tools you need not only to navigate the U.S. visa system but to receive a warm welcome to America as well.

Let's get going!

# PART ONE

# U.S. Visas
# The Basics

# CHAPTER 1

# What is a Visa?

> ## In This Chapter
>
> ➤ Visa defined
>
> ➤ Different kinds of visas
>
> ➤ Applying for a visa
>
> ➤ The terms

In the world of U.S. visa and immigration law, understanding the precise meaning of certain terms is crucial, and perhaps no term is more important to understand than visa.

The word is subject to a great deal of misunderstanding and confusion. Some people think they need a visa when they don't, while others may not have a visa when they think they do. Some people may think a visa is the same thing as permission to remain in the United States indefinitely, whereas the duration of a visa does not govern the duration of time a foreigner may remain in the United States. Some people confuse a visa with a passport, but they are two entirely different documents. A nonimmigrant visa, the type of visa we cover in this book, is not a green card either, nor does it give the holder citizenship.

## Defining Visas

Basically, a visa is a U.S. travel document issued by the federal government. Once the government has reviewed and approved an individual and his or her eligibility to enter the United States, a light blue stamp 4¾ inches wide and 3⅛ inches tall is impressed onto a page of the foreigner's passport. This is the visa. It allows a non-U.S. citizen to present himself for inspection at a port of entry and attempt to enter the United States temporarily for a specific purpose. It's important to know that a visa is only permission to apply to enter the United States; it is not a guarantee that the visa holder will be allowed in.

**Visa Vocab**

A port of entry is a place where customs officials are stationed, such as a border crossing or airport, to check people and foreign goods entering a country.

Confusion comes into play because so many different types of visas are issued for so many different purposes that many people are not sure what rights they actually give the visa holder.

# Variety of Visas

The type of visa we'll be discussing in this book is the nonimmigrant visa (NIV). This is a visa issued by the U.S. Department of State (DOS) to foreign nationals who are coming to work or to visit the United States for a specified period of time. After that time, the beneficiary goes back home. In contrast, an immigrant visa is issued to a foreigner who intends to live in the United States permanently. We will not be covering immigrant visas (except in passing), passports, citizenship, or visas issued by any other country.

**Visa Vocab**

A person holding a visa is called the beneficiary. The terms visa holder and beneficiary can be used interchangeably.

## Each Visa is Unique

A visa is not a blank check. Each type of nonimmigrant visa is governed by its own set of rules and conditions. Certain activities may be permitted in one category that are expressly forbidden in another. For example, a foreigner in the United States with a professional worker visa is permitted to work only for the employer who sponsored him or her for that visa. An individual with a tourist visa, by contrast, is expressly prohibited from working for any U.S. employer or from being paid in the United States. Every visa category comes with different rules. Failing to abide by the specific terms of the visa category can void the visa and make an individual's presence in the United States illegal.

## Alphabet Soup

Visas come in many different flavors, but each is identified by an alphabetic code such as A, B, F, L, or H. A visa to visit the United States for business or pleasure, for example, is a B visa. An executive transfer visa is an L visa.

Within a particular alphabetical category are subsets, such as an L-1A (manager/executive visa) or L-1B (specialized knowledge visa).

The most common nonimmigrant categories are:

➤ B-1: Business visitor

➤ B-2: Tourist

➤ H-1B: Professional worker

➤ L-1A: Multinational executive*

➤ L-1B: Specialized knowledge worker*

➤ O-1: Aliens of extraordinary ability

*Also known as intracompany transferee visas

### Example Please

A common visa (in this case an R-1 visa) looks like this:

As you can see, this visa (like most nonimmigrant visas) carries certain identifying features. Specifically, the visa carries a photo of the individual; the individual's name, nationality, and date of birth; the visa type (L-1 in this case); the place where the visa was issued (São Paulo); and the visa's issuance and expiration dates.

The visa may carry certain other annotations, such as the name of the individual's employer (in the case of a work visa) or other important notes such as "no extensions permitted." At the bottom of the visa is a series of encrypted bar codes that carry electronic identification information on the visa and the visa holder.

# The Application Process

Two separate, distinct regulatory agencies govern the admission of foreigners to the United States: the United States Bureau of Citizenship and Immigration Services (USCIS) issues permission to obtain most (but not all) nonimmigrant visas; the DOS actually issues the visas. Within each of those agencies are different divisions.

### Visa Vocab

Outside of the United States, the U.S. embassy is the government institution people go to when applying for a visa. The section of the embassy that issues visas is called the consulate, and the issuing official is called a consular officer, or consul.

The process of admission to the United States generally begins with an application to the USCIS for permission to receive a visa in a particular visa category such as tourist visa or a work visa. There are certain exceptions, however, that may allow you to skip this first step (see chapter 10).

If the application is approved, you then apply at a U.S. embassy for the visa stamp. A consul will review your individual credentials and eligibility, such as by checking your name on a database. If you are granted the visa, you then may apply at a port of entry. A Customs and Border Protection (CBP) officer will then judge your admissibility for admission to the United States.

In some cases, the procedures are even more complex and even more governmental agencies can get involved, but this application process is the basic structure of the U.S. system for admitting foreigners.

## Before You Leave the Embassy

The consular officers who issue visas are human. They deal with thousands of visas a week. Many of the issuing officers are newly trained foreign service officers, whose first unglamorous job is to issue visa stamps. In other words, they make mistakes. Instead of correctly issuing you a professional visa, they may issue you a NATO employee visa in error. These mistakes happen all the time.

Unfortunately, you as the visa holder bear the brunt of their mistakes. Remember, you have to show this visa to a U.S. immigration inspector at a port of entry to be queried on the purpose of your visit. If your visa stamp has a picture of a Chinese woman and you are a tall blond citizen of Germany, you can expect to spend several hours in a small room speaking with U.S. government officials. Similarly, if your visa is annotated "prohibited from employment," and you arrive and tell the immigration inspector, "I am here to work," you are in for a long day at the airport.

The lesson is simple: look at your visa before you leave the embassy. Read it. Make sure it is correct.

### The CBP

It is fundamental to understanding the system that you appreciate that the U.S. immigration inspector, the CBP official, has unfettered discretion to deny entry to any applicant. The inspector may challenge the validity of the visa or the basis on which the visa was granted. The inspector may even cancel the visa if he or she believes the basis of its issuance was fraudulent. The inspector has the final word.

#### Example Please

As a sort of cheat sheet, the responsible agencies and their functions are as follows:

USCIS: Visa petitions

DOS: Visas

CBP: Admission to the United States

While CBP has the discretion to admit or deny anyone, as a practical matter, the inspector will not look behind the validity of a visa in the great majority of cases. What he or she will do, however, is ask a series of questions to confirm in his or her mind that the basis of entry is consistent with the visa at issue. Unless there is a glaring irregularity or some other exigent circumstance, the visa is usually sufficient to permit entry.

# Know Thy Visa

Knowing the terms of your visa is critical. If you entered the United States as a tourist and you waited tables after you arrived, you have violated the terms of your visa. It does not matter that your visa is facially valid. As a result of your activities, the immigration authorities will deem you to be here illegally or, in their terms, "unlawfully present." This can have draconian consequences.

#### Example Please

A foreigner with a diplomatic visa may be asked by a CBP inspector what he or she will be doing in the United States. If the answer is inconsistent or contradictory to the visa at issue, the inspector could send the foreigner to secondary inspection for additional interrogation.

Knowing what your particular type of visa allows you to do (and prohibits you from doing) is critical to staying out of immigration trouble.

## *Expiration*

Perhaps the single most important piece of information about a visa is the expiration date. When a visa expires, it cannot be used to reenter the United States, just as an expired passport cannot be used to travel abroad. It does not mean that the visa necessarily has to be replaced or renewed or that the holder is no longer permitted to remain in the United States. Many foreign visa holders who do not travel abroad stay in the United States perfectly legally with expired visas provided they have maintained legal status (see chapter 3), a critical distinction.

Now that we have covered the visa fundamentals, let's discuss some fundamental distinctions: Immigrant vs. nonimmigrant visas, and visa vs. status.

### **Advice of Counsel**

Simply because a visa has not expired and is valid does not mean the individual is in the United States legally. The duration of the beneficiary's stay is governed by his or her status as evidenced by his or her arrival and departure record (see chapter 3).

# CHAPTER 2

# Immigrant vs. Nonimmigrant Visas

## In This Chapter

➤ Immigrants and nonimmigrants

➤ The immigrant intent issue

➤ Dual intent

The first key distinction to understand when navigating the murky waters of U.S. visa law is the difference between the terms *immigrant* and *nonimmigrant*. Despite the technical jargon, the distinction is really quite simple.

# Immigrants

An immigrant is a resident from another country who either has or is in the process of obtaining lawful permanent residency (LPR) in the United States. This is a legal status for which a green card is issued.

An immigrant who has been deemed to be an LPR will be so for life and is entitled to a variety of benefits such as blanket permission to work in the United States, as well as some detriments such as being deemed a U.S. resident for federal tax purposes.

### Visa Vocab

A green card identifies a foreign national as a permanent resident of the United States.

A green card is the physical card issued when LPR status is acquired. It may expire or become lost or stolen and need to be renewed, but the LPR status of the immigrant is still in effect provided he or she maintains certain time periods of residency in the United States or otherwise doesn't give up his or her immigrant status. In other words, permanent residency is exactly that—permanent.

### Visa Vocab

An immigrant visa is a specific one-time travel permission that triggers someone's LPR status.

### Visa Vocab

A nonimmigrant visa is a short-term, temporary visa to enter the United States for a specific purpose. Every foreigner who enters the Unites States legally without a green card or an immigrant visa is by definition a nonimmigrant.

## *Immigrant Visas*

As part of the process of obtaining LPR, the applicant is issued an immigrant visa. This is in most cases the final stage of the LPR process. Once the individual enters the United States with an immigrant visa, he or she becomes a permanent resident.

# Nonimmigrants

A nonimmigrant is someone who is not an immigrant or a U.S. citizen and is not entitled to remain permanently in the United States.

The distinction between immigrant and nonimmigrant is more than mere semantics. The concept of temporariness touches nearly all areas of visa law and, importantly, colors how the government looks at nonimmigrant visas (NIVs) and the people who apply for them. The U.S. government usually wants to see specific and definitive evidence that a person applying for an NIV intends a temporary visit for a specific and temporary purpose. Failure to prove this to the government means the visa will not be issued.

### Advice of Counsel

One's U.S. legal status can be categorized as:

➤ U.S. Citizens: May permanently reside in the United Sates

➤ Immigrants: May permanently reside in the United States

➤ Nonimmigrants: May temporarily reside in the United States

➤ Illegal foreign nationals: Unclear

The key distinction is how long an individual in each category is permitted to live in the United States. For U.S. citizens and immigrants, the answer is forever; they have permanent residency.

## Nonimmigrant Visas are Temporary

A nonimmigrant visa status is specific to a purpose and a time frame. This temporary vs. permanent distinction underlies the entire visa system, as will become increasingly clear.

NIVs permit the holder to enter and remain in the United States for a temporary period and for a specific purpose. The period and the purpose will vary depending on the NIV at issue. A B-2 tourist visa, for example, will permit someone to enter the United States for up to six months at a time but will not allow the individual to be paid or employed while in the United States. An L-1A (multinational manager or executive) visa, by contrast, may permit someone to remain in the United States for up to seven years and will permit them to work for the company that sponsored them for the L visa but not for anyone else. Each NIV category is different. The most common categories will be discussed further in the chapters to come.

## NIVs Are Organized by Letters

Each NIV is identified by a specific letter of the alphabet. These designations are important, because each category has its own set of rules, guidelines, time frames, and so forth. An expert who hears the term *E visa* will immediately know that it relates to international trade or investment and that the holder may work in the United States for an extended period of time. By the same token, an expert who hears *B visa* will know the holder is a business visitor or tourist and is not permitted to work in the United States (subject to some specific exceptions, which we will discuss). In short, each letter is a code that represents certain general attributes about the visa it represents. The numbers represent whether the holder is the principal applicant or a dependent. The principal applicant usually has a *1* beside the letter (such as L-1A), while the dependent will have a *2* (such as L-2).

### Example Please

Where do the alphabetic designations for visas come from? What do they mean?

The Immigration and Nationality Act, which created the various visa categories, is subdivided into various sections. The alphabetic designations refer to the letter used for each specific category. For example, business visitor visas are known as B visas because they are defined in the act's subsection as (a)(15)(B). Intracompany transferee visas are known as L visas because they are defined in section 101(a)(15)(L). That's all these designations mean. If the various nonimmigrant visa categories were dealt with in a different order in the law, they would be known by different letters.

The following are the key characteristics of NIVs:

➤ NIVs are temporary visas

➤ NIVs are not green cards—they do not entitle the holder to remain in the United States permanently

➤ Each NIV category is designated by a letter of the alphabet

➤ That letter represents the legal reason that visa holder is permitted to be in the United States, for what purpose, and for how long

➤ Each type of NIV has different rules regarding one's purpose and length of time allowed in the United States

# Immigrant Intent

One requirement of most NIV applicants is to demonstrate that they do not have what is called immigrant intent and want to remain in the United States indefinitely. The U.S. government wants to believe that if it grants an NIV, the nonimmigrant will return to his or her native country when the period of permitted stay expires.

A consular officer who is assessing the immigrant intent of someone who is applying for an NIV must determine the applicant's subjective state of mind. Will the applicant seek permanent residency, or will he or she leave the United States when the NIV status expires?

### Visa Vocab

A U.S. consular officer is an official appointed by the government to live in a foreign country and represent the commercial interests of U.S. citizens.

## *Why Immigrant Intent Matters*

How does this come into play in the real world? When you apply for a visa, the consular official will evaluate your case and make an assessment of your immigrant intent. If the official believes you are an intending immigrant, you will not get your visa. Period. Proving that you do not have immigrant intent is absolutely critical to whether the consul will grant you a visa or not. This is especially critical for those applying for B visas. In fact, the law has an express presumption that B visa applicants are intending immigrants, and it is your job to overcome this presumption.

---

**Example Please**

In many countries, particularly in poorer nations, the immigrant intent barrier can be pretty high. This is true especially for individuals perceived as having a high degree of intent (or ability) not to return home. For example, those who are young and single are perceived as having more immigrant intent than those older or with spouses or children (especially when their spouses or children are staying behind while the principal applicant visits the United States). Similarly, executives with established jobs in their home country, such as lawyers, will be perceived as having less immigrant intent than those with more transient or less stable jobs, such as dishwashers.

---

### *Overcoming the Intending Immigrant Presumption*

How would one prove a lack of immigrant intent? The State Department wants to see that the applicant has "a residence outside the United States as well as other binding ties that will ensure their return abroad at the end of the visit." Some kinds of evidence the consul looks for might include:

➤ A letter from your employer attesting that you have a job in your native country to which you will return

➤ Deeds for property that you own

➤ Evidence of money or bank accounts

➤ Proof of family members remaining behind in your native country to greet you upon your return

The degree of required evidence of not having immigrant intent varies from country to country depending upon the perceived flight risk of the country and the person in question. For example, a married, middle-aged business executive from Germany will have an easier time obtaining a tourist visa than will a young, single unemployed teenager from Brazil.

Obviously, the issue of an applicant's intent is not only highly subjective, but also may be difficult to assess. What if you don't know whether you intend to live in the United States in the future? What if your intent changes?

# Dual Intent

Not all NIVs need to prove immigrant intent. A few specific employment-related NIVs—specifically the L-1 (intracompany transferee), H-1B (professional worker), and O (alien of extraordinary ability) visas—permit the applicant to have what is called dual intent. As the name implies, dual intent means that these specific visa holders may in fact have two different intentions: nonimmigrant intent, meaning they intend to leave once their temporary visa is up, and immigrant intent, meaning they intend to obtain a green card and stay indefinitely.

### Visa Vocab

Dual intent is a legal concept that a visa applicant may have two intentions at the same time: a short-term intent to leave the United States and a longer intent to stay. This means that for those visa categories that permit dual intent, the consul will not use the immigrant intent issue as the basis to deny a visa.

## *Why Dual Intent Matters*

As you have no doubt figured out, it is generally easier to apply for an NIV in a category that permits dual intent because you will not be faced with the intending immigrant presumption. Or to put it more bluntly, a category with dual intent gives you a loophole to avoid the issue of immigrant intent altogether.

If you are in the United States with an NIV that requires you not have immigrant intent, you may be technically unable to apply for a green card while in that status. After all, the basis for the visa was that you were not an intending immigrant. The fact that your intent might have changed is irrelevant. This is why the dual intent concept is so critical to the L-1, H-1B, and O-1 NIV categories, which permit dual intent. In many cases, NIV holders of visas that do not permit dual intent have no opportunity to move from an NIV status into permanent residency.

### Advice of Counsel

The dual intent distinction has evolved because most applicants in the NIV categories that permit dual intent have been executives or white collar workers, many of whom wished to remain in the United States as green card holders. Consequently, exemptions developed for these visa categories. (To complicate things further, one category, the E (investor) visa category, does not specifically recognize dual intent but permits it in certain circumstances—don't ask).

## *Choose a Category with Dual Intent (If You Can)*

To summarize, depending on the category, proving a lack of immigrant intent is crucial. How crucial will again depend on the NIV category. For the B (tourist) visa, it's the whole ball game. If you are unable to overcome the presumption that you have immigrant intent, you will not get the visa. For other visas, such as the F (student) visa, the presumption remains, but it generally is enforced less strictly than with the B visa. Finally, for the NIV categories that expressly recognize or permit dual intent, there is no issue.

For individuals who might be eligible for more than one NIV category, it's a no-brainer that they would want to choose a category that permits dual intent. That way they keep all of their options open.

By the same token, other NIV holders who aren't so lucky and who want to remain in the United States on a longer-term basis may have to pursue a strategy of switching their status from one NIV category (say, F) to another (say, H) to take advantage of the dual intent loophole.

Understanding the immigrant intent issue and whether it applies to your particular visa category is absolutely crucial to your success in navigating the visa process. If you put yourself in the shoes of an immigration inspector or a consular officer responsible for issuing you a visa and understand that they are looking at you through the lens of immigrant intent, you will be able to muster your evidence and state your case accordingly.

# CHAPTER 3

# Visa vs. Status

## In This Chapter

➤ What is status?

➤ How status is granted

➤ The I-94 card

➤ I-94 is a work permit

In the previous chapter we discussed the difference between immigrants and nonimmigrants, and we explored what a visa is and what it is not. We also noted the common misperception that having a visa (even a valid visa) makes you legal in the United States. The truth is a little more complicated. That brings us to the difference between visa and status.

## The Interrelationship Between Visa and Status

Does a visa give you status? Yes and no. The two concepts—*visa* and *status*—are intertwined but separate, like two heads of a coin or yin and yang.

### Visa Vocab

Your status is the legal designation of the conditions under which you are present in the United States as indicated by the type of visa you have.

### Advice of Counsel

If you are legally in the United States and behaving in accordance with the terms of your visa, you are said to be *in status*. If you are violating the terms of your visa—or have overstayed the period of permitted stay—you are said to be *out of status*. Legal visitors have status; so-called illegal immigrants don't have status. Status is what separates the two.

A visa is the tool that enables you to apply for status, just as an airline ticket enables you to board a plane. However, status itself is only granted once an immigration inspector admits you to the country. You would not get status without the visa (usually), but once you have status, it exists whether you have a visa or not.

Confused? Let's examine how this works and return to the visa we looked at in chapter 1:

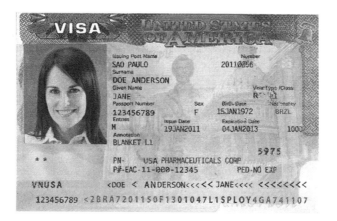

As you can see, the visa contains pertinent biographical information about its holder— name, date of birth, nationality, and the like. Importantly, it also carries on its face an NIV designation; in this case it's L-1. The L-1 distinction is shorthand for intracompany transferee. The NIV designation tells a government official what the parameters are for the holder's permitted entry into the United States and what the holder is allowed to do.

# How Status is Given—Mrs. Doe Flies to Washington

Let's assume Mrs. Doe, the holder of the L-1 visa shown above, intends to fly from São Paulo to Washington to start work for her L-1 employer. Earlier she received the above L-1 visa

## Visa Vocab

The I-94 card is the form issued by the federal government that tells you what your status is and how long it remains valid. Put differently, it is the I-94 card, not your visa, that states how long you may remain legally in the country.

from the U.S. consulate in São Paulo. When Mrs. Doe checks in at the airport for her flight, the airline representative looks at her visa and confirms that on its face it appears valid. (Note that the representative does not look at the bona fides of the visa or inquire further beyond the fact that she has a facially valid visa—after all, that's not the rep's job).

The airline official—either when Mrs. Doe checks in or more likely on the flight itself—hands Mrs. Doe a white form to fill out called an I-94 arrival and departure record. Many times the flight attendant hands this out along with the customs forms.

The I-94 card looks like this:

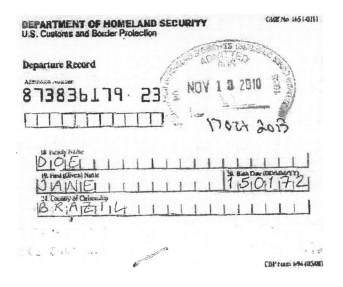

Note that the I-94 card is white. This is very important. There is a green version of the form as well, which is otherwise basically identical, called I-94W. This is the form that's used for those without a visa who are entering on the Visa Waiver Program. We will talk about this in more detail, but for now, if you have a visa stamp—meaning you went to an embassy and were given a visa—you fill out the white version of the I-94 card.

### Advice of Counsel

Airline officials are not experts on these matters and can hand out the wrong forms by accident. If Mrs. Doe fills out the green I-94W card by accident, rather than the white I-94, she will be inspected and admitted as a ninety-day visitor under the Visa Waiver Program, in which case she can under no circumstances work and must depart within ninety days despite the fact that she has a valid visa.

## Questioning by the Immigration Inspector

Once Mrs. Doe lands in Washington, she collects her carry-on baggage from the overhead compartment, and then drags herself down a corridor toward a long line of dour, uniformed immigration inspectors.

Once her name is called, the immigration inspector looks at four things to determine if Mrs. Doe is eligible to be admitted to the United States as a nonimmigrant visitor.

First, the inspector checks her passport—mainly to confirm her identity and ensure her name doesn't appear in a master database of criminals or terrorists.

Second, if Mrs. Doe has not done so already, she is (generally) photographed and registered as part of the United States Visitor and Immigrant Status Indicator Technology (US-VISIT) system. In some places this is done at a kiosk, at others with a small camera when facing the inspector. Note that Mrs. Doe has to do this only once, the first time she enters the United States. Once she is in the system this step is no longer required.

Third, the inspector reviews Mrs. Doe's visa. After all, the visa is the permission slip that allows her to enter the United States. The fact that she has a visa tells the inspector that the DOS has already run a check on Mrs. Doe's identity and confirmed that, at least from its perspective, she was eligible to obtain a visa. It also means her name did not trigger any DOS watch lists.

Upon reviewing her visa, the immigration inspector asks her the purpose of her trip to confirm that her answers comport with the facts as shown on her visa.

Mrs. Doe is an employee of USA Pharmaceuticals Corp.—this is clearly shown on her visa. (The visa was also granted as an L Blanket, which is not important for now but will be discussed in chapter 9). Therefore, the inspector is likely to request confirmation from her about the terms of her employment.

**Visa Vocab**

Employers apply for or sponsor most nonimmigrant visas and all employment-based NIVs. The employer is sometimes called the petitioner since technically it is the entity that has applied for the visa on behalf of the employee. The individual visa holder is known as the beneficiary since he or she benefits from the application.

For example, in Mrs. Doe's case the exchange might go something like the following:

Inspector: "What is the purpose of your trip?"

Mrs. Doe: "I work for USA Pharmaceuticals Corporation."

Inspector: "What do you do?"

Mrs. Doe: "I'm the CFO."

The inspector might also ask about the nature of her job, or where the company is located—basic facts. But in the case of most work-related nonimmigrant visas, such as Mrs. Doe's, the inspection will not go much beyond these sorts of fact-checking questions.

It is critical that Mrs. Doe's answers line up with the information on her visa. The inspector does not have much time to go beyond the basic information shown on the visa so if the correct answers are given, the inspection process usually ends.

If, however, Mrs. Doe answered Baker Biotech when asked who she worked for when her visa clearly says USA Pharmaceuticals Corporation, more questions or even a secondary inspection may be called for.

Finally, the immigration inspector looks at her I-94 card, stamps it with a date, and writes the visa designation, in this case L-1, on it. The date stamped on the I-94 card for an L-1 visa will probably be three years from the date of admission, which is the permitted length of time one can enter the United States on an L-1A visa initially.

## *Voila! Status is Granted*

Once Mrs. Doe walks away, she has status—specifically, L-1A nonimmigrant visa status. The I-94 card—duly annotated by the inspector—is evidence of this status.

What does this mean? This means she has legally been admitted to the United States and is permitted to remain in the country through the date given on her I-94 card—in this case, October 17, 2013. The fact that she now has status also means that she is permitted to engage in any activities permitted by this status, in this case to work for and be paid by USA Pharmaceuticals Corporation in the role of CFO.

What about her visa? It no longer matters, at least as far as her legality while in the United States is concerned. Her visa has fulfilled its function—it has gotten Mrs. Doe through inspection and allowed her to receive the all-important I-94 card denoting her status. Mrs. Doe could lose her visa (and her passport for that matter). Or her visa could expire. But provided she has a valid I-94 card, it does not matter—her status is legal. (Of course, losing her passport and visa would create other, different problems.)

### Advice of Counsel

If you are eligible, you can file a petition with the U.S. Citizenship and Immigration Services (USCIS) to extend or change your status. If you are eligible, and USCIS agrees, it will send you a new I-94 card via mail. See chapters 19, 20, and 21 for more details on how this works.

# I-94 Card Trumps Visa

If Mrs. Doe overstays the date on her I-94 card, she is out of status and thus in the United States illegally even if her visa remains valid. The only date that matters in terms of whether a person is here legally or illegally is the date on the I-94 card. This date trumps the visa.

In short, so long as Mrs. Doe remains in the United States, her L-1A visa stamp is wholly irrelevant to what she does or whether she is legal. This is governed by her I-94 card once she enters the United States.

### I-94 Card Gives Permission to Work

By receiving the I-94 card, Mrs. Doe was given something else: work permission.

Foreign visitors often ask about how to get a work permit for the United States. Technically, there is no such thing. Permission to work in the United States comes in one of three flavors:

> ➤ A green card

> ➤ An employment authorization document (EAD) (see chapter 23)

> ➤ A I-94 card (for nonimmigrant visa holders)

Once Mrs. Doe has been admitted in status, her I-94 card is proof of her eligibility to work (assuming she was admitted in a category where work is allowed—as was true in her case). Along with personal identification, such as a passport, the I-94 card is sufficient for Mrs. Doe to prove she is legally eligible to work for her U.S. employer, a process known as completing an I-9 form. Put another way, the I-94 card is her work permit.

# When Status Exists—And When It Doesn't

Status exists only when an individual is physically present in the United States. If you leave the United States—poof!—status "magically" disappears.

Similarly, in the eyes of the government status exists by virtue of behavior appropriate to the visa category. If, for example, you are admitted with a B (tourist) visa (and thus are ineligible to work) and you get a job waiting tables, you are technically out of status. Does the government know this? Of course not! Nevertheless, your status has magically disappeared (at least in the government's eyes) even though your I-94 card may still be valid on its face.

## *The Holy Grail of Visa Law*

Immigration lawyers are often faced with bizarre situations due to the vagaries of the I-94 card. For example, the immigration inspector writes the wrong date on the I-94 card, stamping an earlier year. Or suppose Mrs. Doe was given an I-94 card that was good for only twenty-four hours—or even backdated by accident to before the date she was inspected? Could such things happen? Of course—they happen all the time.

In such a case, is Mrs. Doe out of status and therefore illegally present? The answer is yes. But it's not her fault! Too bad.

The inspector could write down the wrong visa category—B instead of L-1. Then Mrs. Doe would technically have B status and would not be eligible to work. Or the principal applicant might be given three years of status, but his wife and kids are given only one year. Or a person might lose his I-94 card. Or a person's visa might expire, but his I-94 card is still valid and he has to travel abroad. Problem: without a valid visa, there is no basis to apply for status again at the port of entry. The I-94 card is deemed to be infallible. Whatever it shows—even if it was done in error—is the correct legal status. These issues arise every day, and immigration lawyers spend a great deal of time correcting them.

Maintaining and preserving status is the Holy Grail of immigration law. If a person has correct and valid status, most issues and problems can be corrected, even if doing so is difficult. Status can be extended or changed, but only if status is not lost. Individuals out of status, on the other hand, whatever the reason, have many more problems.

Status, like innocence, once lost is nearly impossible to regain.

# PART TWO

# The Process Explained

# CHAPTER 4

# Step One: An Approved Visa Petition

## In This Chapter

➤ An overview of the process

➤ How to apply for an approved petition

➤ Approval! The I-797 form

➤ Denial

By way of brief but vigorous review, thus far we have learned the following:

➤ A foreign national needs a visa to enter the United States for most purposes (and for all employment purposes) unless he or she has a green card.

➤ A visa is simply a travel document issued by the U.S. government—specifically, a travel document issued by consulates of U.S. embassies in various nations around the globe.

➤ A temporary visa, or nonimmigrant visa, entitles you to enter the United States for a temporary period and for a specific purpose. Once admitted, you are a nonimmigrant—as opposed to an immigrant, who is a permanent resident of the United States.

➤ Visas come in all different flavors, each with its own rules about what is permitted.

➤ Finally, a visa is important to get you into the United States, but once you are allowed in, it is your status (as shown on your I-94 card), not your visa, that governs your ability to remain legally in the United States.

Those are the basics. Now that you understand them, the next question is how do you get a nonimmigrant visa?

# A Multistep Process

As we touched on earlier, obtaining a visa is generally a multistep process. This is certainly true of all employment-based visas, such as the L-1A (multinational executive) and H-1B (professional worker). As we also saw, several different agencies of the United States federal government are involved in the process of applying for and obtaining NIVs.

Let's assume that you wish to apply for a standard employment-based visa such as an L-1A intracompany transferee visa. Don't worry about the specific requirements of the L-1A—we will address those in chapter 9. The step-by-step process of obtaining an L-1A is substantially similar to many other NIVs, so this will give us a good overview.

### Advice of Counsel

Only consulates located outside of the United States issue visas. If you are in the United States with another type of visa or without a visa (because you were eligible for a visa waiver), you will have to leave the United States, obtain your visa, and then reenter. There is no other way to obtain a visa.

# Obtaining Preapproval

The L-1A visa requires that you obtain preapproval with USCIS before you are eligible to apply for a visa at a consulate. This preapproval is known as an approved petition. Technically, it's the I-797 form. In the top right corner of the form next to "Notice Type" are the words "Approval Notice." This is to differentiate it from a different notice, such as a denial. The underlying forms all look the same. The way you tell them apart is by looking at the section that tells you what type of notice it is.

### Advice of Counsel

Almost all NIV categories require an approved petition for the consul to adjudicate a visa application. The four most common exceptions to this rule are the B-1 (business visitor), B-2 (tourist), E-1 (treaty trader) and E-2 (treaty investor) visas. The B and E categories fall within the specific jurisdiction of DOS and therefore no approved petition is required. For that matter, even if you have an approved petition in B or E cases, the consul will review your case from scratch, as if you didn't have one.

The consul will not usually review the underlying criteria for the L-1A visa petition. Once USCIS issues an approved petition, the consul will assume that the criterion for eligibility for the visa (meaning the legal criteria, such as in the case of an L-1A visa whether the individual works for an overseas affiliate of a U.S. company) was satisfied.

So step one of many NIVs, including L-1A visas, is applying for and (hopefully) receiving an approved petition from USCIS. This is the basis for your L-1A application at a consulate abroad.

# The Application Process

The process for applying for an approved petition is fairly straightforward, although the underlying documents and forms can be complicated. In the case of a standard L-1A petition, you would send the following forms to USCIS for approval:

> ➤ I-129—the basic NIV application form

> ➤ I-129 L supplement—an additional form that is specific to the L-1 visa application

> ➤ A letter from the petitioner (the employer) describing the basis for eligibility for the L visa. This is usually drafted by counsel to the petitioning company, for the letter must clearly spell out the legal basis for the case.

> ➤ Supporting information and documentation about the employer and the application, such as an annual report in the case of public companies

> ➤ A copy of your passport information

> ➤ The applicable filing fees

The above represents—in broad strokes—the paperwork necessary to apply for an approved petition for an L-1 visa from USCIS. Most other nonimmigrant visas require this paperwork as well as other evidence specific to the type of visa. For example, an H-1B (professional worker) visa requires evidence different from that of an L-1A (multinational manager or executive) visa, although both require an I-129 form to be submitted.

## A Cautionary Note

As you might imagine, the filing standards and requirements are very specific in each case. Failure to submit the correct form or fill it out correctly will result in the case being rejected and sent back to the petitioner. While the basic form for all petitions is the I-129, other supplemental forms are required based on which kind of NIV you are requesting. For example, there is an L supplement form for L visas (I-129 L supplement), an O supplemental form for O visas (I-129 O supplement), and so forth.

Most of the information required at this stage relates to your employer, the nature of your job, and the legal basis for the visa. Other than some general information related to you (name, nationality, and DOB), the petition process has very little to do with the individual. That comes during the visa interview/application process, which we will discuss in the next chapter.

### Advice of Counsel

The level of detail and nature of supporting documentation required varies for each case and each NIV category. Consult the USCIS website for the specific filing requirements for the petition you are applying for, or have an immigration lawyer do it for you. The forms are complicated and change regularly, so answering the questions as specifically and correctly as possible—in addition to making sure you have included everything required for that particular visa category—is absolutely critical.

# Where and How to Apply

The application forms, supporting evidence, and filing fees are mailed to one of four government processing facilities in Vermont, Texas, California, or Nebraska, depending on where the petitioning company is located. The process is entirely impersonal and done by mail, unlike the visa process, which is done in person. There will not be any personal interview, or for that matter any direct communication with the service center, unless it requests additional evidence or have questions.

## *The Receipt Notice*

Once USCIS receives your application, it will send you a form acknowledging it. This is called a receipt notice and gives you certain information about your case, in particular a specific code that allows you to track your application's progress either online or by calling USCIS. Again, it looks very much like the other notices you might receive, but you will know it is only a receipt from the fact that it says this in the top right corner under "Notice Type."

Department of Homeland Security
U.S. Citizenship and Immigration Services

I-797C, Notice of Action

## THE UNITED STATES OF AMERICA

| RECEIPT NUMBER WAC-11-030-51054 | CASE TYPE  I129 PETITION FOR A NONIMMIGRANT WORKER |
|---|---|
| RECEIVED DATE November 15, 2010 | PRIORITY DATE | PETITIONER COMPASS GROUP USA INC |
| NOTICE DATE November 16, 2010 | PAGE 1 of 2 | BENEFICIARY PAGE, CHRISTOPHER ROBERT |

Jane Doe
322 E. 77th Street
New York, NY 10075

Notice Type:   Premium Processing
Receipt Notice
Amount received: $ 1320.00

Thank you for choosing to use the U.S. Citizenship and Immigration Service's Premium Processing Program. The above petition or application has been received and accepted as a Premium Processing case. You should receive a notice regarding your case within 15 days from the date shown on the received date above. If the Service needs to contact you regarding your case they may do so by mail, telephone, facsimile or e-mail using the information you provided.

Please notify us immediately if any of the above information is incorrect.

If you need to contact us regarding your Premium Processing case you can do so using the information immediately below. The mailing address, e-mail address and phone number listed below are for use in relation to cases filed under the Premium Processing Service program only. You can obtain your status information from our automated system 24 hours a day with a touch-tone phone and the receipt number for this case shown above by calling the phone number listed below

CALIFORNIA SERVICE CENTER (CSC) Premium Processing

Routine Mail: P.O. Box 10825, Laguna Miguel, CA 92607-

Courier delivery Address: 24000 Avila Road, 2nd Fl., Room 2302, Laguna Miguel, CA 92677

I-129 PP Fax: 949-389-7486
PP Phone Number: 1-866-315-5718

Email box: CSC-Premium.Processing@dhs.gov

This notice does not grant any immigration status or benefit. It is
not even evidence that this case is still pending. It only shows that the application or petition was filed on the date shown.

**If this case is an I-130 Petition -**. Filing and approval of a Form I-130, Petition for Alien Relative, is only the first step in helping a relative immigrate to the United States. The beneficiaries of a petition must wait until a visa number is available before they can take the next step to apply for an immigrant visa or adjustment of status to lawful permanent residence. To best allocate resources, USCIS may wait to process forms I-130 until closer to the time when a visa number will become available, which may be years after the petition was filed. Nevertheless, USCIS processes forms I-130 in time not to delay relatives ability to take the next step toward permanent residence once a visa number does become available. If, before final action on the petition, you decide to withdraw your petition, your family relationship with the beneficiary ends, or you become a U.S. citizen, call 800-375-5283.

**Applications requiring biometrics.** In some types of cases USCIS requires biometrics. In such cases, USCIS will send you a SEPARATE appointment notice with a specific date, time and place for you to go to a USCIS Application Support Center (ASC) for biometrics processing. You must WAIT for that separate appointment notice and take it (NOT this receipt notice) to your ASC appointment along with your photo identification. Acceptable kinds of photo identification are: a passport or national photo identification issued by your country, a drivers license, a military photo identification or a state-issued photo identification card. If you receive more than one ASC appointment notice, even for different cases, take them both to the first appointment.

**If your address changes.** If your mailing address changes while your case is pending, call 800-375-5283 or use the

Please see the additional information on the back. You will be notified separately about any other cases you filed.

Form I-797C (Rev. 01/31/05) N

# What Happens Next?

The processing time for a petition depends on the type of case it is. Certain cases, such as fiancé visas, simply take longer than others to adjudicate. It also depends on how busy USCIS is at that particular moment and which service center is reviewing the petition (some are simply more efficient than others).

In any event, review of your case will not happen overnight. The processing time for most run-of-the-mill cases can take between three and six months. Therefore, plan ahead in terms of your timing and expectations. Don't plan to obtain a visa in one week if you haven't even filed the petition.

### Advice of Counsel

For an extra filing fee of $1,225 for premium processing, USCIS is required to adjudicate the petition fifteen calendar days from the date of receipt.

# Approval! Form I-797

Once USCIS reviews your petition, one of two things happens. Your petition is approved, in which case you'll receive an approval notice in the mail. This approval notice is the basis for you to apply at a consulate to obtain your visa. A typical approval notice looks like this:

---

Department of Homeland Security
U.S. Citizenship and Immigration Services

I-797A, Notice of Action

## THE UNITED STATES OF AMERICA

| RECEIPT NUMBER | CASE TYPE | |
|---|---|---|
| WAC-11-030-51054 | T129 PETITION FOR A NONIMMIGRANT WORKER | |
| RECEIPT DATE November 15, 2010 | PRIORITY DATE | PETITIONER John's Dress Shop |
| NOTICE DATE November 17, 2010 | PAGE 1 of 1 | BENEFICIARY Jane Doe |

Jane Doe
322 E. 77th Street
New York, NY 10075

Notice Type: Approval Notice
Class: L1A
Valid from 12/15/2010 to 12/14/2012

The above petition and extension of stay have b_____ _____ the named foreign worker(s) in this classification is valid as indicated above. The foreign worker(s) can work for the petitioner, but only as detailed in the petition and for the period authorized. Any change in employment requires a new petition. Since this employment authorization stems from the filing of this petition, separate employment authorization documentation is not required. Please contact the IRS with any questions about tax withholding.

The petitioner should keep the upper portion of this notice. The lower portion should be given to the worker. He or she should keep the right part with his or her Form I-94, Arrival-Departure Record. This should be turned in with the I-94 when departing the U.S. The left part is for his departure records. A person granted an extension of stay who leaves the U.S. must normally obtain a new visa before returning. The left part can be used in applying for the new visa. If a visa is not required, he or she should present it, along with any other required documentation, when applying for reentry in this new classification at a port of entry or pre-flight inspection station. The petitioner may also file Form I-824, Application for Action on an Approved Application or Petition, with this office to request that we notify a consulate, port of entry, or pre-flight inspection office of this approval.

The approval of this visa petition does not in itself grant any immigration status and does not guarantee that the alien beneficiary will subsequently be found to be eligible for a visa, for admission to the United States, or for an extension, change, or adjustment of status.

THIS FORM IS NOT A VISA NOR MAY IT BE USED IN PLACE OF A VISA.

Please see the additional information on the back. You will be notified separately about any other cases you filed.
U.S. CITIZENSHIP & IMMIGRATION SVC
CALIFORNIA SERVICE CENTER
P. O. BOX 30111
LAGUNA NIGUEL CA 92607-0111
Customer Service Telephone: (800) 375-5283
Form I797A (Rev. 09/07/93)N

PLEASE TEAR OFF FORM I-94 PRINTED BELOW, AND STAPLE TO ORIGINAL I-94 IF AVAILABLE

Detach This Half for Personal Records

Receipt # WAC-11-030-51054
I-94# 798892115 21
NAME   Jane Doe
CLASS  L1A
VALID FROM 12/15/2010 UNTIL 12/14/2012

PETITIONER:            INC
        John's Dress Shop
        1005 Second Avenue
        New York, NY 10065

798892115 21

Receipt Number WAC-11-030-51054
Immigration and
Naturalization Service
I-94
Departure Record       Petitioner:

| 14. Family Name | |
|---|---|
| Doe | |
| 15. First (Given) Name | 16. Date of Birth |
| Jane | 06/24/1970 |
| 17. Country of Citizenship | |
| UNITED KINGDOM | |

**Visa Vocab**

An approval notice is not generic to visas generally; it is visa specific. The type of visa you have been approved for is printed on the notice's face and the consul will know by looking at it what type of visa USCIS has approved for you.

As you can see, the I-797 says that the petition was approved by USCIS and gives the NIV category you are eligible to apply for (here, an L-2). The fine print on the form describes the process and that you now may use the approval to obtain your visa.

Congratulations—you have made it over the first obstacle to receiving a visa.

# Denial

If you are unfortunate, you will receive a negative response from USCIS. This will come in one of two flavors. First, if you have forgotten a specific form, or USCIS has additional questions about your case, it will mail you a notice of intent to deny (NOID) form. As the name suggests, this means the government intends to deny your case unless you can provide additional evidence as to why it should be approved. This notice contains follow-up questions about your case or asks for specific information you may have failed to provide.

**Visa Vocab**

A notice of intent to deny is called a kickback in the industry.

If USCIS reviews your case and concludes that you are not eligible for the visa, you will get a rejection notice.

A denial is USCIS's final answer that you cannot apply for this type of visa, at least based upon the case you presented in that petition. A denial sometimes follows a kickback if you fail to adequately answer the additional questions USCIS asks you.

A petition can be denied for many reasons: failure to properly complete a form, substantive ineligibility for the category, etc. The USCIS has broad discretion to approve or reject a petition, although USCIS is obligated to explain its rejection in a denial.

## Example Please

The fact that the notice is a rejection is set forth in the top right corner. This looks like the following:

| Department of Homeland Security U.S. Citizenship and Immigration Services | | | I-797C, Notice of Action |
|---|---|---|---|

**THE UNITED STATES OF AMERICA**

| ReceiptNumber | | Case Type: | |
|---|---|---|---|
| MSC-11-103-17885 | | I-130 - Petition for Alien Relative | |
| Received Date: | Priority Date: | Petitioner: A043741105 | |
| January 10, 2011 | | John Smith | |
| Notice Date: | Page 1 of 1 | Beneficiary: A200365661 | |
| January 12, 2011 | | Jane Doe | |

NOTICE TYPE: Rejection Notice

```
Jane Doe
322 E. 77th Street
New York, NY 10075
```

The application/petition you filed along with any fee you submitted is being returned to you for the following reason(s):

    X    The check amount is incorrect or has not been provided. The correct filing fee is $420.00. Please resubmit the application/petition with the appropriate fees to the address listed on the bottom of this notice.

If you need additional assistance, please contact the USCIS National Customer Service Center (NCSC) at 1-800-375-5283. For TDD hearing impaired assistance, please call 1-800-767-1833.

If you have Internet access, please visit the United States Citizenship and Immigration Services website at www.USCIS.gov for further information.

U S BUREAU OF CITIZENSHIP AND IMMIGRATION SERVICES
P.O. Box 805887
Chicago, IL 60680-4120
National Customer Service Center: 1-800-375-5283

5584968          0558496803          Form I-797C (Rev. 12/28/09) Y

A denied petition does not mean that the individual is not permitted to enter the United States in another visa category or even to reapply. It simply means that with respect to that specific application, the underlying criteria were not sufficiently proven.

Once you receive the I-797 form, you are more than halfway toward your goal of receiving the visa. Now it is time to prepare for the application at the embassy.

## Advice of Counsel

For most NIV cases, this two-step process of USCIS approves the petition and DOS issues the visa is the norm. But there are a myriad of exceptions and caveats to this general structure.

To give but a few examples:

➤ Before an H-1B petition can be filed with USCIS, another approval, called a labor condition application (LCA) must be obtained, a sort of preapproval to the preapproval. This is not terribly difficult or complex, but it involves a third governmental agency, the Department of Labor (DOL).

➤ An E visa can be applied for either by filing a petition with USCIS or by applying directly with the embassy. However, the embassy will give a USCIS approval little or even no weight and will readjudicate the case.

➤ Certain nationalities (Canadians, for example) are visa exempt. This means they can travel on the approved petition itself, without the need to obtain a visa at all.

# CHAPTER 5

# Step Two: Applying at the

## In This Chapter

➤ Who has to apply

➤ What you submit

➤ Where you apply

➤ When you apply

➤ Why you might have issues

As we have seen, an approved petition is needed for a U.S. consul to give you a visa in most cases. For some visas, such as the widely used B visa, no petition is required—you simply apply directly at the consulate. But whether an approved petition is required, whether the visa is employment based, whether you are in Bavaria or Bolivia, the fundamental process of attaining a visa is the same.

Every visa applicant fourteen to seventy-nine years of age is required to apply in person for their initial visa stamp. The process for making an appointment varies from consulate to consulate, but it generally can be done online or by phone. During your appointment you will submit certain forms and filing fees. You may or may not be asked many questions, but in most employment NIV cases, the questions will largely be confirmatory. Based on your application, the consul will (or will not) issue you a visa stamp. That is the process in a nutshell.

**Advice of Counsel**

With limited exceptions, every applicant for a visa between the ages of fourteen and seventy-nine is required to apply for a visa in person. An applicant may be permitted to renew a visa in the same category via mail without a second interview—it depends on the consul.

Although the fundamental process of attaining a visa is the same no matter the NIV or consulate, the details such as where you apply, what paperwork you must submit, and so forth vary from case to case and country to country. To understand the process in detail, let's break it down into the five *W*'s: Who, What, When, Where, and Why.

# Who

Who must apply for a visa? As we saw, any foreign national wishing to seek admission to the United States must apply for a visa to enter the United States, unless that foreign national

> ➤ has permanent residency in the United States,

> ➤ is eligible to enter without a visa pursuant to the Visa Waiver Program (see chapter 18),

> ➤ is visa exempt because he or she is from a NAFTA country (see chapter 12).

There are some additional exotic exceptions that we won't discuss here.

### Visa Vocab

The applicant, generally meaning the individual on whose behalf an approved petition was issued, is called the principal or beneficiary—the latter because he benefits from a visa petition filed on his behalf by his employer, or sponsor. (In nonemployment-based cases, a sponsor may also be an individual.) The spouse and children of the beneficiary are called dependents.

### Advice of Counsel

Only the principal is required to have an approval notice. His dependents are not required to have separate approval notices for an initial issuance of a visa, although they might be required to have separate approval notices for extensions to show that they have maintained status while in the United States.

# What

What are you required to submit? It depends. As we have touched upon, there is a range of NIV categories based on certain employment categories, family relationships, or other status. Some of these visas (L, H-1B, O) require approved petitions while others (E, B) do not.

What you are required to submit depends on the NIV you are applying for as well as the consulate. While the requirements of each consulate vary from country to country, the standard requirements are as follows:

> ➤ Original I-797 approval notice: This is needed only if required for your visa as evidence that your petition has been approved by USCIS. Again, certain visas do not require this, although most do.

> ➤ Original appointment confirmation letter: When you schedule your appointment at the consulate, it will generally issue you a letter confirming the time and date of your appointment. This is the permission slip to enter the consulate.

> ➤ DS-160 nonimmigrant visa application form: The DS-160 is the standard visa application—every applicant worldwide must complete this form to apply for an NIV.

> ➤ Visa application fee receipt: Most NIV applicants are required to pay a fee. The exact amount varies by the type of NIV but is commonly in the range of $150. This may not be the only fee required, however; it depends on the type of visa and the consulate. Check carefully exactly what fees are required in your case and how to pay them. Some consulates are very particular about the payment system, and failure to make the payment correctly will result in a delay in issuing your visa.

> ➤ Passport photos of each applicant

> ➤ Supporting documentation: This varies based on the type of NIV. For example, a B visa applicant is required to produce evidence regarding immigrant intent, whereas an L-1A applicant will not.

> ➤ An original passport for each visa applicant: The passport must be undamaged and with sufficient pages to insert the visas. It must also have an expiration date at least six months in excess of the expiration date of the visa.

The above are the general requirements. Now let's flesh out some of the details.

## *The DS-160 Form: Required Everywhere*

The DS-160 is an online form that must be submitted to DOS by almost every person applying for a nonimmigrant visa. Certain exceptions are made for some of the more exotic visa categories, such as the S (aliens assisting in law enforcement), T (victims of human trafficking), and U (victims of crime), which require a different form.

Personal information, such as DOB, parents' names, education history, and travel history, is required for the DS-160 form. This information is fed into a DOS database to check whether the applicant is listed on any international databases for criminal activities, such as terrorism.

### Visa Vocab

The DS-160 form is required of every NIV applicant regardless of age and visa category. The form is easily found online, either at the DOS website (http://travel.state.gov/visa/forms/forms_4230.html) or at the consulate where you'll be applying for your visa.

There is not a lot of magic to completing the DS-160 form, although the questions sometimes require longer answers than the space available to complete them. Answer every question. Write down your answer even if it's "none" or "N/A." Certain questions, such as listing every country you have visited in the last ten years, may require additional space. If necessary, type this on a separate sheet of paper. You may not know the answer to some questions, such as what your future travel plans are, but use your best judgment. The form can now be completed online using electronic signatures. Remember that every family member applying for a visa is required to complete this form, even the youngest of children.

Each consulate has its own processes and procedures to complete the DS-160. Check your consulate's requirements.

### Advice of Counsel

If you have retained a visa service or lawyer to assist you, they should be able to guide you through the specific consulate requirements. Otherwise, check the consulate website carefully and read all of the documentation that it sends you when you book your visa appointment. Nothing trips up more visa applications than the filing fees and photographs. Remember, this is the government you are dealing with, and the rules can be bureaucratic and pedantic. If you get something wrong, a delay will result.

## *Photos and Fees*

The passport photographs you are required to submit must be taken in accordance with prescribed rules and dimensions. Your head must face a certain direction, the photos must be of a certain size, and so forth. Check the exact requirements for the photos online and make sure yours comply. If you are in doubt, take extras with you.

Similarly, check the exact fee schedule for your visa category and your consulate. Many NIVs have a reciprocity fee in addition to the visa application fee noted above. Check what this fee is and how to pay it. Certain consulates require that you pay certain fees ahead of time (such as at preapproved banks), and bring a receipt with you. If you don't plan ahead for this, you won't have the receipt and your application will not be complete. Also, consulates generally do not take credit cards—bring extra cash and checks with you in case there is an additional fee you did not anticipate. Bear in mind that every applicant, not just the principal, must pay the visa application fee.

## Paperwork

The supporting documentation required varies based on the type of NIV at issue. If you are married or have children, a good rule of thumb is to always bring an original copy of your marriage certificate with you, as well as your children's birth certificates. If you have an approved petition, also bring a copy of the underlying filing, in addition to the I-797 form. Seek advice of counsel if you are in any doubt about what is required, and always check the consulate's website for current updates and procedures.

OK—so you've completed your paperwork and double-checked your forms. What happens next is usually anticlimactic.

If your paperwork is correct and thorough, it should make the case for you. Although you are required to attend the appointment in person, there is generally not an interview per se. Particularly in cases of an approved petition, you will likely only be asked some confirmatory questions, such as your name, your intended dates of travel, your address, and so forth. In B visa applications the questions may be more searching as they are required to assess your immigrant intent. Stay calm, answer the questions correctly and briefly, and when in doubt, have the interviewer refer to the paperwork and supporting documentation you have submitted. Most of these questions should have been addressed in your filing.

# Where?

Where do you apply? The easy answer is you should apply at the consulate that has jurisdiction over the area where you live.

## Residency

If you live in Paris for example, you would apply at the American consulate in Paris. Some countries might have several different consulates that issue visas. In Brazil, for example, there are four consulates where you might apply for a visa, depending upon what part of the country you live in: Brasília, Recife, Rio de Janeiro, or São Paulo. If you live in Great Britain, you have to apply in London. You can easily find which consulate has jurisdiction for your case by checking the DOS website.

Do you have to be a national of the country in which you are applying? What if you are a French national living in Panama? Can you apply in Panama, or do you have to return to France? Generally, you are permitted to apply in the country in which you are residing, or even in a country you happen to be passing through.

### Visa Vocab

Applying for a U.S. visa in a country in which you are not a resident is called third country processing, and the applicant is called a third country national. This is generally permitted, but it depends on the particular consulate and the nature of the NIV at issue.

## *Third Country Processing*

Most consulates permit third country processing if the reason for your physical presence in the country is legitimate and the NIV application is not problematic. If, for example, you are a European national temporarily on vacation in the Bahamas, the Bahamian consulate will generally take your case. The consuls give preferential processing times and appointments to home country nationals, however, meaning that the processing time for third country nationals can sometimes be longer. In addition, if the reason you're in the country is suspect or if your case has substantive or procedural problems, the consul may refuse to take it and require that you apply in your home country.

### Advice of Counsel

While permitted, third country processing should be treated cautiously. Depending on the type of case and the nationalities involved, the case might be delayed or the consulate might decline to take it.

Consulates are sensitive to situations where an individual might be perceived as consulate shopping, meaning they're applying in a jurisdiction seen as more favorable to a review of the case. Also, if a case has been previously denied by one consulate (particularly a home country consulate), a third country consulate will generally refuse to take it.

# When?

When should you apply for your visa? As soon as you are ready and, in particular, well in advance of the time you require your visa. If you intend to begin work in the United States on Monday, do not schedule an appointment that day (or even the Friday before) expecting that you will have your visa in hand. Visa issuance is not immediate. Generally the consulate will receive your application and issue your visa a day or so after—sometimes as much as a week later. Sometimes it's returned by mail or express delivery, which can also add a day or so to the processing time. This is the government after all, so do not expect same-day service.

### *Use Your Common Sense*

Calculate the time of year in which you are applying. Most people travel either toward the end-of-the-year holidays or in mid-summer. The consulates are flooded with applications at both of these times of year and by the same token, consulate staff is more likely to be working reduced hours or be on vacation. Use common sense in making your travel arrangements, and build in extra time for contingencies if something goes wrong such as missing a form or having paid an incorrect filing fee.

Double- and triple-check that you have included all of the relevant forms and have answered all of the questions. A minor mistake may cause additional delays of several days.

If you require your visa the same day due to legitimate circumstances—such as a personal or business emergency—ask the consular officer if it's possible to expedite your case. Bring a letter or other evidence regarding the nature of the emergency. This doesn't guarantee your visa will be issued any quicker, but it doesn't hurt to ask.

Finally, show up on time or early, if possible, and expect to wait. Don't be late and assume that the government will understand and accommodate you. Bring a magazine to read. Do not bring any electronics, phones, or other devices. The consulate might not let you in, and in any event this will delay your appointment. Check the consulate website for what is allowed or disallowed in the building.

# Why?

Hopefully, you won't need to ask "why," since this question comes up mainly when a visa application has been denied. If your case has been denied, the consul is obligated to give you an explanation, which usually comes in the form of a printed letter, sometimes as a standard form. The basis of denial comes in two categories:

➤ A paperwork or technical error can be the cause of denial. Perhaps your passport photograph has the wrong dimensions or you forgot to pay the reciprocity fee or to include your I-797 form. These types of errors are generally fixable, although they delay the application, so try to avoid them in the first place.

➤ A rejection related to your substantive ineligibility for a visa or something particular to you specifically, such as personal ineligibility (prior arrests, drug use, etc.) is more problematic.

For example, B visa denials usually relate to immigrant intent—in other words, you did not overcome the presumption that you are an intending immigrant.

There can be many reasons for a denial. Read the denial letter carefully, as it will tell you exactly the basis for the consul's decision. If you are denied a visa, we recommend you consult counsel. It might be a simple or innocent mistake (either yours or theirs), in which case it should be quickly fixed. Or it might be something more serious, in which case you will need counsel to get it resolved.

# CHAPTER 6

# Step Three:
# Admission to the

---

## In This Chapter

➤ Entering the United States with an employment NIV

➤ Entering the United States with a tourist visa (or under visa waiver)

➤ The special case of the business visitor

➤ What to do if things go wrong

---

You survived your interview. You received your passport back from the consul with a shiny new visa stamp in it. You have your airplane ticket, and you are ready to go. You are ready to seek admission to the United States.

What should you expect? How should you prepare?

Well, to a large degree it depends on which visa you were issued—or whether you were issued a visa at all.

---

### Example Please

The technical term for being allowed to enter the United States once you have spoken with an immigration inspector is *admission*. When you have been given an I-94 card and have passed through immigration and customs, you have been admitted to the United States with a nonimmigrant status.

# Being Admitted with an Employment-Based Visa

If you were granted an NIV, such as an L-1 (intracompany transferee), O-1 (aliens possessing extraordinary abilities), or H-1B (professional worker), you can relax in most cases. The hard part is over. If your visa is valid and correct, admission should not be a problem unless you have specific issues such as a prior arrest, in which case there will be an annotation on your visa, and the CBP officer will likely want to ask you additional questions.

## Advice of Counsel

An ounce of prevention is worth a ton of cure. A week or so before you travel, double-check that your passport is valid and your visa stamp is correct. Read it carefully for any errors. Have any family members coming with you do the same with theirs. Bear in mind the validity period of your passport must be six months past the date of your expected entry into the United States for most nationals (UK citizens and many EU nationals are currently exempt from this rule, although this could change).

Your NIV is good evidence that the government has scrutinized your case and found that you are worthy of admission. While the immigration inspector will want to confirm that the period and validity of your visa is accurate, generally that will be the extent of the questioning.

## Visa Vocab

The term *immigration inspector* technically refers to a customs and border protection (CBP) agent at a port of entry.

## *What to Bring With You*

When entering the United States, you can't know which documents you'll be asked to produce, so it's better to have everything with you. For example, suppose your name triggers a red flag in the entry system and you're pulled for secondary inspection and additional questioning. In such a case, supporting evidence that your visa was validly issued would be good to have with you. Admittedly, this would be an unusual case—but it's always better to have more documentation and not need it than need the documentation and not have it. So be sure you have the following documents with you:

➤ A copy of your approved petition (the I-797 form) and all supporting documentation

➤ A copy of your marriage license if you're entering the United States as a couple. This is particularly true if you do not share the same surname

➤ A copy of birth certificates for any children entering the United States

➤ A copy of your passport and visa stamp

# Being Admitted with a Tourist Visa or Visa Waiver

If you have a business visitor visa or tourist visa, your situation is slightly different. Although the consulate has issued you a visa, the inspection process can be more rigorous. Specifically, the inspector needs to ensure that the basis of your entry is legitimate (meaning you are not working and your visit is temporary) and that you do not have immigrant intent. Keep the following in mind when speaking with an immigration inspector. This advice goes for entry under the visa waiver rules as well.

➤ Tell the truth. Answer all questions honestly and do not make any misrepresentations. Every problem except fraud can be fixed. Give simple, straightforward, and clear answers to all questions.

➤ Remain calm and courteous. Remember the immigration inspectors are only doing their job. They are required to make a decision in approximately sixty seconds as to an individual's eligibility to enter the United States. It is often easy for an immigration inspector to misunderstand circumstances or misconstrue facts. Therefore it is important that you do not provide too much information, but at the same time you need to respond to questions in a clear and concise manner.

➤ Understand that immigration inspectors are not attempting to deny your entry when they ask you questions. They are not asking trick questions; they are simply attempting to determine the basic reasons for your desire to enter the United States.

➤ Remember that as an NIV temporary visitor you must demonstrate that you intend to leave the United States within a reasonable period of time, that you will not be employed while in the United States by any U.S.-based entity, and that you will not provide any productive employment services to U.S.-based customers or clients.

➤ You must demonstrate that you have a home outside of the United States and intend to return to your home abroad. The questions immigration inspectors ask you are predicated upon determining your intent and the temporariness of your visit. Once you understand this, you will know what questions are coming and how to accurately answer them.

## *What to Have on Hand*

In addition, for those entering as tourists or business visitors, we recommend that you bring the following documents with you to support your basis for entry. You may or may not be asked for them, but it is certainly advisable to have them with you.

> ➤ A return plane ticket demonstrates that you intend to leave the United States. Should you have an open ticket, you need to be able to articulate when you anticipate leaving the United States and the reason why you have not yet confirmed your departure date.

> ➤ Evidence for the purpose of your trip. For example, if you're entering to engage in business meetings, bring a letter to this effect from your foreign employer. Have a copy of your business cards and a confirmation from the hotel you are staying in.

> ➤ If you are a tourist, have a copy of your itinerary and evidence of where you will be staying as well. The more documentation you have, the better. You may not be asked to produce any of it—and in fact in most cases you will not—but in the rare instance when you are, you will be glad that you have it.

## *Remember the Word* **Temporary**

As we have discussed, one of the criteria for NIV holders is that the basis of the visit is temporary. The longer you are in the United States, the greater the presumption may be that you are working in the United States.

There is no cutoff time for what is considered temporary, but the longer or the more frequent your visits, the greater scrutiny you will receive when you are entering with a B visa or under visa waiver.

### Advice of Counsel

If you are a frequent visitor to the United States, be prepared to explain why. For example, following hurricanes in the Caribbean several years ago many executives of international companies in the Cayman Islands were forced to visit the United States frequently while major business functions were temporarily relocated to Florida. In those cases, visitors explained that due to the recent hurricanes in the Caribbean, they were traveling more often to Florida until operations were fully up and running back home. This gave a clear, truthful, and understandable explanation to the inspectors, who might otherwise have wondered why an individual was coming in and out of the United States every several months. Truth is the best defense.

# The Special Case of the Business Visitor

Business visits, whether with a B visa or under visa waiver, can be particularly tricky. Not only do you have to overcome the intent issue, but in addition you have to make clear that you are not working or employed while in the United States. In this case, getting the terminology correct and giving an explanation is critically important.

## Tips to Keep in Mind

Reiterating the basic facts—and certain legal distinctions—is critical. For example, you need to communicate the following clearly to the immigration inspector (assuming, of course, all of this is true):

➤ You are employed outside of the United States and will be visiting the United States in conjunction with your duties and responsibilities abroad.

➤ You are not going to be employed in the United States.

➤ You will not receive any compensation from any U.S. source.

➤ You will not be servicing U.S. customers or clients, and you will not be engaged in productive employment services while visiting the United States.

➤ You intend to leave the United States upon the conclusion of your visit and return to your home abroad and your place of employment. (This goes to the intent issue.)

➤ Avoid references to or words such as *working* or *employed*. While this might be ordinary language that makes sense, unfortunately an immigration inspector may misconstrue or misinterpret these statements and view them literally, which may then unfortunately render you ineligible to visit the United States for business.

➤ Avoid any statements that leave the duration of your visit open-ended. For example, you should not indicate to an immigration inspector that you do not know when you will be leaving the United States. You should also not indicate that you are unsure if you will remain in the United States in the future. Again, this speaks to intent.

**Advice of Counsel**

Bear in mind that these guidelines apply only to visitors entering with B visas or under visa waiver. If you have an employment NIV, the above issues regarding immigrant intent do not apply to you.

These subtle but important distinctions can be the difference between an easy admission process and one fraught with difficulties.

# What to Do if Things Go Wrong

Despite the best preparation, things can go wrong. Perhaps you didn't communicate well, perhaps the inspector simply does not know what he or she is doing. Whatever the reason, if things do not appear to be going well during your inspection process, bear in mind the following:

> ➤ Don't panic. Do not allow yourself to feel pressured into admitting in any way that you are not a legitimate visitor for business. On occasion, immigration inspectors can have a rough questioning style. Do not allow an immigration inspector to intimidate you into taking the next flight back home.

> ➤ If you have immigration counsel, have them prepare a letter on your behalf that explains why your visit is legitimate and permitted. If you find yourself in difficulties with the inspector, politely advise the immigration inspector that your attorneys specifically analyzed the circumstances under which you are visiting the United States and have determined that you have a legitimate basis to visit. Show him or her the letter. In a real bind, and assuming your counsel agreed to this, politely recommend that the immigration inspector call your counsel directly in order to clarify any facts or circumstances relating to your visit to the United States. (That almost never happens, by the way.)

> ➤ Don't worry should the immigration inspector ask you to sit in a secondary inspection area or room. Unfortunately, you may be required to wait several hours as a result of this secondary inspection process, but it in no way means that you will not be admitted to the United States as a visitor. Stay calm—ask if you can speak with your lawyer.

> ➤ You may encounter an immigration inspector who says, "I will let you in this time, but I do not want to see you again soon." Don't attempt to argue with the inspector. These words are meaningless and have no bearing on your ability to reenter the United States as a visitor provided your circumstances continue to remain legitimate for a temporary business visitor.

A senior lawyer we knew had a great saying: Prior Preparation Prevents Piss-Poor Performance. Nowhere is this truer than in the admission process.

# PART THREE

# Temporary Visas for Business

# CHAPTER 7

# Business or Pleasure: The B Visitor Visa

## In This Chapter

➤ For business visitors

➤ Work defined in the visa world

➤ For tourists

➤ Applying for a B visa

Without question, the workhorse of all the nonimmigrant visas is the B visa. It is most requested because of its scope and flexibility. Covering those who are traveling either for business or for pleasure, the B visa leaves little else for other visas to address.

## The B-1 Business Visitor Visa

The B-1 visa is designed to permit a business visitor to enter the United States. It encompasses a wide variety of permitted business activities: making sales calls, attending board meetings, engaging in negotiations, and pursuing business development activities. In fact, the B-1 visa permits nearly any legitimate business activity—provided that the activity does not involve employment or work and the individual is not being paid by a U.S. entity for his

**Visa Vocab**

The B visa comes in two flavors:

➤ The B-1 visa for business visitors

➤ The B-2 visa for tourists

or her services while in the United States. What constitutes employment or work is not as straightforward as it may seem, however.

### Advice of Counsel

The permitted period of entry under a B-1 visa is generally six months unless the visa is specified to be valid for less time. While an immigration inspector has the authority to grant less time than this, generally six months is the norm. The duration of your visa will depend upon what nationality you are and the length and purpose of your trip.

## Permitted Activities with a B-1 Visa

For business visitors who need to enter the United States but do not qualify for the Visa Waiver Program, which allows people of specified countries such as the United Kingdom, France, and Australia to travel in the United States without a visa, the B-1 visa is usually the visa of choice.

It would be pretty difficult—if not impossible—for the U.S. federal government to make an exhaustive list of all the possible legitimate business reasons a foreigner might have to visit the United States. These would range from visiting clients to attending a seminar to negotiating a contract. The possibilities are nearly endless, so any business reason that does not involve a foreign national engaging in work or being paid while in the United States (subject to certain exceptions discussed below) should in theory qualify for a B-1 visa.

### Visa Vocab

*Work* is a term that allows interpretation in the B-1 visa context. Generally, activities that look and smell like labor constitute work—and almost any activity that results in payment from a U.S.–based employer while the individual is physically present in the United States constitutes work—but not always.

### Permitted Reasons for a B-1 Visa

While there is no all-encompassing list of permitted activities that fall under the B visa umbrella, regulations do contain certain activities that consular officials are advised are appropriate and legitimate reasons to grant B-1 visas.

Examples of business activities that are expressly permitted under the B-1 visa include:

➤ Engaging in commercial transactions, such as negotiating contracts

➤ Engaging in litigation

➤ Attending meetings with clients or business associates

➤ Participating in scientific, educational, professional, or religious conferences

➤ Taking orders and performing technical services under existing service or sales contracts

➤ Undertaking independent market or product research on behalf of a foreign company

➤ Settling an estate

➤ Setting up an investment, such as opening back accounts or incorporating a business

➤ Attending board of director meetings

Some other professional activities that are less common but that have been permitted under the B-1 visa are:

➤ Playing professional sports, such as golf or motorsports, provided the individuals receive no salary (only tournament money)

➤ Preaching on an evangelical tour if supported by contributions

➤ Engaging in work-related activities that would also qualify for an H-1B (professional worker) visa provided the individual is not paid in the United States

## Domestic Servants of U.S. Citizens

In addition, domestic servants such as nannies and cooks who work for U.S. citizens are eligible for a B-1 visa if their employers permanently live abroad and are returning for a brief visit or have been temporarily reassigned back to the United States.

### Advice of Counsel

The substantive purposes for which you may be permitted to enter the United States under a B-1 visa are exactly the same as those permitted under the Visa Waiver Program. So in most cases where an individual would qualify for a visa waiver (most Europeans, Japanese, and a few other nationals), there is usually no need to obtain a B-1 visa. These individuals can simply enter the United States without a visa for exactly the same business purposes.

### Domestic Servants of NIV Holders

Domestic servants of most nonimmigrant visa holders are also eligible for B-1 visas, but additional restrictions apply. In this case, employees must show all of the following:

➤ They are not abandoning their foreign residence

➤ They have worked for their employer for one year, or they have ongoing employment with that employer and have at least one year's prior experience as a servant

➤ They have an employment contract stating that they will be paid the prevailing wage by the employer

The domestic servant exceptions noted above are exceptions to the general rule. Overall, any legitimate business activity is permitted under the B-1 visa provided the individual is not being paid by a U.S. entity or source, the purpose of the trip appears temporary, and the individual is not working in the United States.

# What is Work Anyway?

How *work* is defined? This question is more difficult to answer than you might first think. Clearly, coming to the United States to work in your uncle's restaurant washing dishes for the summer would qualify as work. In fact, the immigration rules specifically define *work* as local employment or labor for hire.

But think about some less obvious examples.

Isn't an accountant coming to the United States to help conduct an audit labor for hire? Wouldn't that be considered work? What about a lawyer working on a transaction in the United States or a sales technician repairing a machine? Aren't these people working?

Arguably yes, although in both cases the individuals would almost certainly qualify for a B-1 visa provided they were not being paid by a U.S.-based employer while in the United States.

## A Fine Line

Why would these cases be permitted but other cases not?

There is no clear answer. What constitutes prohibited work (or labor for hire) versus permitted business activities can be pretty subjective. Each case is analyzed on its own merits, and the consular officer simply makes a call as to whether the visit looks like work or looks like a business visit. So does a CBP officer upon inspection for admission to the country.

## *Factors to Determine What Is or Is Not Work*

That being said, there are a few concrete factors the consular officer looks at when deciding whether an activity constitutes work or not.

> ➤ Time. How long is the visit to the United States? A four- to six-week visit to engage in meetings on a discrete project looks like a temporary business visit. An open-ended, multi-month assignment looks more like work.

> ➤ Purpose. Does the purpose look like one that would normally require a work visa? For example, is the individual running a manufacturing line or managing the accounting function of a U.S. corporation? In those cases, one could argue that a visa would be necessary to conduct these activities. But they veer into the area of work if the basic activities have the look and smell of labor, especially manual labor. On the other hand, discrete and defined activities are appear more legit.

> ➤ Job Shopping. This practice developed as a way of certain industries to bring in foreign workers (in many cases Indian or Chinese) to work in the United States without obtaining employment visas, in most cases because they were not eligible for them. The foreign worker would be paid outside the United States but essentially sent "on loan" to a U.S. employer for a six- to twelve-month period. Job shopping scenarios—or activities that look like this—are not permitted. This is especially true in certain industries (IT) or for certain nationalities (Indian, Chinese) that immigration authorities are particularly sensitive to—situations where it appears that a B-1 visa is being used as a vehicle for the individual to work in the United States without a true employment visa. Again, a good rule of thumb is that if the activity looks and smells like work, the visa will not be issued.

If the above analysis sounds extremely subjective—it is. This is why obtaining B-1 visas can be a tricky matter and require the applicant (or representing lawyer) to explain why he or she is not working when in fact, at least in some generic sense, it could be argued that he or she is.

### Advice of Counsel

The U.S. consular official making the decision whether to grant you a B-1 visa has only limited information to go on, usually a brief letter from you or your employer explaining the nature of the trip. Based on this, he or she will have to make an entirely subjective determination as to whether or not your trip looks like work. Being clear about your purpose and using correct terminology can mean the difference between denial and approval.

## Why Are Servants Exempt?

It might have occurred to you to wonder why domestic servants are permitted to obtain B-1 visas. Aren't domestic servants working and, for that matter, even being paid in the United States? Why are these activities permitted under B-1 visas?

The short and unsatisfying answer is: that's simply the way it is. The regulations make a specific exemption for domestic servants.

If that's not a satisfactory answer, you have to bear in mind that the rules that govern the issuance of visas have been forced over time to adapt to the realities of actual people and their needs. Some NIV holders needed to bring their domestic servants to the United States with them, and there wasn't a visa category that really applied. So, the government rewrote the rules to make a specific exception for domestic servants. It could, in theory, have created a separate visa category, but it didn't. There is no logic to it, that's just how it is.

# The B-2 Tourist Visitor Visa

The B-2 tourist visa is a bit simpler to comprehend than the B-1. In theory, any legitimate non-business-related purpose is eligible for a B-2 visa. Tourism is the most obvious purpose, but there are many other reasons that are generally found to be legitimate, such as health care visits, visiting relatives, or attending special functions (such as a musical or artistic festival or performance). Sometimes a visit may include both business and tourism.

Suppose you intend to visit the United States for business meetings, but you also plan on doing some sightseeing while you are in New York. Which visa is right for you—the B-1 or the B-2? The answer depends upon what is the primary purpose of your trip. In the example above the primary purpose is to attend business meetings, so the appropriate visa is the B-1. As a practical matter, almost all activities permitted under one category are permitted under the other—in other words, you are not required to obtain both a B-1 visa and a B-2 visa for a trip where you will mix business with pleasure.

## People Not Eligible for B-2 Visas

While there is not a set list of approved B-2 activities, there is a definitive list of people who are generally not eligible. In addition to job shoppers or other individuals who may be deemed to be working in the United States, the rules provide that the following individuals are generally not eligible for B-2 visas:

➤ Any individual with a preconceived, but undeclared, intent to remain in the United States and seek change of status to longer-term, employment authorized, nonimmigrant classification—in other words, anyone in the consular official's opinion who doesn't seem to intend to return home.

➤ Any individual who is eligible for a visa within a separate category, such as a student (F) or journalist (I). Again, the theory is that if a specific NIV category exists for your job or purpose, it's more appropriate for you to apply in that category rather than as a catch-all B visitor.

➤ Students taking a course of study that exceeds eighteen hours a week, and individuals attending seminars or conferences for credit toward a degree. The consulate takes the position that these specific and common situations require F (student) visas, not B visas.

# Obtaining a B Visa

Criteria for the B visa are quite straightforward, although the specific documentary requirements will vary from country to country.

### Advice of Counsel

Proving that you do not have immigrant intent is the key to obtaining a B visa. Most B visa applications live or die on this issue.

➤ The applicant must demonstrate a legitimate business or other purpose—such as the need to engage in business meetings or the like.

➤ The nature of the visit must be temporary—less than six months in most cases.

➤ The applicant must have a foreign residence that he or she intends to maintain.

➤ Most importantly, the applicant must demonstrate that he or she does not have immigrant intent (see chapter 2).

## Proof for Application

The key to a successful B visa application is twofold: demonstrating a lack of immigrant intent and proving that the nature and purpose of the trip qualifies for a visa.

In the case of the B-1 visa, a letter from the foreign employer describing the nature and purpose of the trip, that the trip will be temporary and is necessary, and confirmation that the employee will not be paid or remunerated by U.S. sources while in the United States will do the trick.

In the case of the B-2 visa, the consular official is particularly keen on seeing a well-defined and temporary purpose for the trip, and knowing that the applicant has sufficient financial resources to complete the trip. In both cases, a return plane ticket is important.

## Applying for a B Visa Successfully

B visa applications do not require a preapproved petition from USCIS, unlike most employment-related nonimmigrant petitions such as for L (intracompany transferee) and H-1B (professional worker) visas. The applicant must simply apply at the relevant embassy. The specific requirements are set forth on the consulate's website but will generally include the customary application form, fees, and photos, as well as a clear narrative description of the intended visit, including supporting information.

## Do I Need A Lawyer?

In situations where the business or social purpose of the trip is well defined, specific, and temporary, individuals are usually capable of applying for a B visa without specific assistance of counsel. However, be careful. Depending on your nationality, the immigrant intent issue could be extremely difficult to overcome, in which case a lawyer could be critical to a successful application.

Many foreign nationals such as those from the visa waiver countries do not require a B visa at all. In these situations, experienced counsel may be helpful in deciding whether as a matter of tactics it might make sense to apply for a B visa, even if it is not technically necessary. This might make sense, for instance, when visits might exceed six months at one time. The visa waiver only permits visits of less than ninety days, so in this case a B visa might be a practical necessity.

Although simple in concept, the B visa is fraught with potential hang-ups—but none more important than overcoming the presumption of immigrant intent.

# CHAPTER 8

# The Camel of the Visa World: The H-1B Professional Worker Visa

## In This Chapter

➤ For business visitors

➤ What makes an occupation professional

➤ The U.S. degree (or its equivalent) requirement

➤ H1-B visa limits

➤ Transferring status to another employer

The H-1B professional worker visa is the most complex of all the nonimmigrant visas. Rules govern how much an employer must pay an H-1B visa holder; how much the visa will cost (depending on how many employees the employer has); which jobs are specialty occupations and thus eligible; and how many visas may be issued by the government in one year. And each of these rules has myriad exceptions, caveats, and subrules. In short, the H-1B visa category is byzantine, bureaucratic, and bewildering. It is also expensive—in some cases, the filing fees alone for an H-1B can run as high as $3,550.

## Visa by Committee

There is a saying that a camel is a horse designed by committee. If that's true, the H-1B visa is the camel of the NIVs—a visa designed by not one but three branches of the federal government:

➤ The DOL, who preapproves the visa through what is called a labor condition application (LCA)

➤ USCIS, who approves the H-1B petition (based in part on the LCA)

➤ The DOS, who issues the actual visa stamp itself

Even congress gets involved by determining how many H-1B visas can be issued each year—what is known as the cap.

**Visa Vocab**

In visa parlance, the cap refers to the number of new H-1B petitions USCIS is permitted to issue for each federal fiscal year, which begins October 1. Once the allotment for a year is reached, no more H-1B visas are available. There are certain exceptions to the cap. Of the NIVs, only the H-1B visa has such a quota system.

# Professional Occupations

Before we enter the H-1B labyrinth, however, let's cover the basics. First, the H-1B visa is generally valid for a total of six years. The visa is issued in two three-year increments. If the applicant is applying for a green card and has reached a certain stage in the process, the H-1B visa may even be extended further (even indefinitely) in increments of one or three years. Family members are eligible for H-4 visas but not for work permission.

The H-1B visa category allows a U.S. employer to hire certain foreign nationals in specialty, or professional, occupations.

## What Are Professional Occupations?

A professional occupation is one that requires the professional to have a U.S. bachelor's degree or other credential to perform the specific job. Some clear-cut classic examples of professional job titles and their corresponding degree requirement are:

➤ Accountant; BA in accounting

➤ Engineer; BS in engineering

➤ Chemist; BS in chemistry

➤ Architect; BS in architecture

Certain professionals—such as accountants, lawyers, or engineers—are self-evidently professional in that we commonly think of them as requiring a specific degree. Many professions, however, are on the fringe. Consider job titles such as acupuncturist, pastry sous-chef, chiropractor, dietician, interior designer, librarian, painting restorer, social worker, vocational counselor, or webmaster. Can they be classified as professional?

Perhaps surprisingly, USCIS decided that these jobs are professional in nature and therefore H-1B eligible. Each case is decided on its own merits.

**Advice of Counsel**

Some exceptions to the degree requirement can be found in the H-1B criteria. The H-1B3 visa, for instance, is reserved for fashion models of distinguished merit and ability.

# The Degree Requirement

A job is considered professional if it meets one of the following criteria:

> ➤ A bachelor's degree or higher or its equivalent is normally the minimum entry requirement for the position.

> ➤ The degree requirement for the job is common to the industry, or the job is so complex or unique that it can be performed only by an individual with a degree.

> ➤ The employer normally requires a degree or its equivalent for the position.

> ➤ The nature of the specific duties is so specialized and complex that the knowledge required to perform the duties is usually associated with the attainment of a bachelor's degree or higher.

In straightforward cases (accounting), proving one of the above criteria can be relatively easy. In other cases (painting restorer), however, the employer must amass evidence—such as detailed job descriptions, media articles, testimonials, or industry statistics—proving to USCIS that the job is sufficiently complex and unique that only an individual with the appropriate degree or its equivalent can perform it. This can be difficult.

## A U.S. Bachelor's Degree

Assuming the job itself qualifies for H-1B status, the applicant must qualify as well. In other words, the applicant must have the relevant background to prove he or she is eligible to perform the professional occupation at issue. For example, in the case of the accountant, the applicant would have to show that he or she had an accounting degree.

According to the regulations, you must meet one of the following criteria to be considered working in a professional, or specialty, occupation:

> ➤ You have a U.S. bachelor's degree or higher from an accredited college or university that is specific to the specialty occupation.

> ➤ You hold a foreign degree that is the equivalent of a U.S. bachelor's degree or higher in the specialty occupation.

> ➤ You hold an unrestricted state license, registration, or certification that authorizes you to fully practice the specialty occupation and be engaged in that specialty in the state of intended employment.

> ➤ You have education, training, or progressively responsible experience in the specialty that is equivalent to the completion of a degree, and you have recognition of expertise in the specialty through progressively responsible positions directly related to the specialty.

### *What Degree Relates to Which Job?*

In the case of an applicant with a degree in painting restoration seeking an H-1B to work as a painting restorer, again the nexus between job and degree is pretty clear. But what if the applicant has a degree in baroque art? Or painting? Or chemistry? What degree requirement is appropriate for the job of painting restorer?

Or to use a different example, what degree is required to be a computer programmer? Would it be mathematics? Physics? Engineering?

Sometimes, it simply is not clear—and if it is not clear to us, I can assure you it will not be clear to the government.

In these more difficult cases, the employer must clearly explain the link between the degree at issue and the profession.

# The Degree's Equivalent

To complicate things further, what if the individual does not have a full degree—or even an academic degree at all? In many industries in Europe, for example, skilled artisans and technicians may have completed only a year or two of formal schooling (or none at all), but they have completed rigorous apprenticeships where they learn their craft working side by side with older professionals. This is true in a variety of fields from woodworking to advanced machine operating to wine making.

Let's continue with the painting restorer job example noted above. Suppose that the painting restorer applicant has twenty-five years of hands-on practical experience in the field, has written five books and a dozen articles, and is recognized as the world's foremost authority in Italian frescoes, but does not have a formal accredited degree. Should such an individual qualify as a professional for an H-1B visa even though he or she lacks a degree?

### How to Equate Experience to Education

In cases where the applicant lacks a formal bachelor's degree—or has a combination of university schooling and work experience—USCIS will count three years of work experience as one year going toward a degree in the relevant field. (Generally, bachelor's degrees in most fields take four years to complete.) For example, if the painting restorer had twelve years of relevant work experience, he or she would have the equivalent of a bachelor's degree using the formula noted above.

Simple enough in theory, but how does this work in practice?

To prove this to the government, the applicant must obtain a third-party evaluation from an accreditation specialist attesting that the work experience equates to a particular bachelor's degree. This is true even if the applicant has a foreign degree.

For example, as shown above, a dozen years of work in painting restoration should be equivalent to a degree. To make this assessment, the evaluator needs to review documents such as detailed job descriptions, letters from previous employers, the applicant's resume, and any work-related certificates or specialized training. As you can imagine, this can become quite a complex process, and even then the evaluation may come back negative (meaning the evaluator did not believe the work is equivalent to a bachelor's degree).

Sometimes the evaluation might produce a degree equivalency that does not relate to the job! For instance, the evaluator in the paint restorer example might conclude that the work experience is equivalent to a degree in fine arts or art history—not paint restoration.

#### Advice of Counsel

Picking a reputable evaluator, amassing the evidence to satisfy him or her, and then receiving an evaluation that fits the proper job can be a time-consuming, expensive, and complicated process. And bear in mind that you must do all of this before the case is even filed with USCIS.

# Enter the Department of Labor

Assuming you can verify that your job is classified as professional and therefore qualifies for H-1B status and that you have satisfied the bachelor's degree or its equivalency requirement, you have one more hurdle before you can take your case to USCIS for an approved petition. You must file a labor condition application (LCA) with the DOL.

## The LCA

Despite its similar name, the LCA has nothing whatsoever to do with what was once called a labor certification, which used to be the first step in certain green card applications. An LCA is simply a preapproval from the DOL that the job at issue meets certain wage and benefits requirements in an effort to protect U.S. workers from cheap foreign labor. The LCA is filed through an electronic system called iCERT.

### Visa Vocab

A labor condition application, or LCA, is an attestation an employer makes to the DOL to the wage and working conditions of the prospective H-1B employee.

By filing an LCA, the employer attests that:

> ➤ it will pay the foreign national employee the required wage (the higher of the prevailing wages or the actual wage paid to U.S. workers similarly employed)
>
> ➤ the foreign national's employment will not adversely affect the working conditions of U.S. workers similarly employed
>
> ➤ there is no strike or lockout that has necessitated the hiring of the foreign national
>
> ➤ notice of the hiring of the foreign national has been provided to the company's employees.

## H-1B Dependency

An H-1B-dependent employer is one whose number of H-1B employees compared to its overall workforce exceeds certain thresholds set by the H-1B rules. The government believes this type of employer is dependent on H-1B foreign workers—not a good thing.

Pursuant to the Soviet-named American Competitiveness and Workforce Improvement Act of 1998, there are several additional attestations for employers to make who are deemed H-1B-dependent employers. They must certify to the DOL that the following attestations are true:

> ➤ They did not displace and will not displace a U.S. worker employed by the employer within a certain time frame.
>
> ➤ They will not place an H-1B worker with another employer who owns, operates, or controls one or more work sites where the H-1B owner performs duties in whole or

in part.

> ➤ They have made good faith efforts to recruit U.S. workers using industry-wide standards and offering prevailing wages.

> ➤ They have offered the position to any U.S. worker who applies and is equally or better qualified than the H-1B worker.

Employers must offer H-1B nonimmigrants benefits and eligibilities for benefits, including participation in health, life, disability, and other insurance plans; retirement and savings plans; and bonuses and stock options on the same basis and in accordance with the same criteria offered to U.S. workers.

Finally, employers are required to maintain DOL-related documents in a secure location called a public access file for public inspection by the DOL.

Employers usually get nervous when reviewing the attestations required by the DOL on LCA and related filings. In reality, however, the DOL plays no real substantive role or function in the H-1B petition process. Unless the job is paying a disproportionately low wage, or some other bureaucratic snafu occurs, the LCA will simply be approved in the ordinary course, a copy put in the public access file, and the paperwork filed away.

You might ask yourself why the H-1B requires an LCA when other NIVs such as L-1A (intracompany transferee) and E-2 (treaty investor) do not. It is a good question, and one with no clear or coherent answer.

Whatever the reasons, the entire DOL/LCA process is little more than an administrative inconvenience created by Congress to protect U.S. workers from cheap foreign labor. (Whether it actually accomplishes this is, of course, open to debate.) A more meaningful barrier—also unique to the H-1B visa—is the so-called cap.

# The Cap

Put simply, Congress puts a limit, or cap, on the number of H-1B visas that USCIS is permitted to issue each federal fiscal year. Since 2002, the cap has been at 65,000.

The importance of the cap is that new H-1B visa petitions (not extensions or change of employers, and not including beneficiaries) must be filed before the annual quota is hit. Where the cap is an issue, the earliest permitted filing for an October 1 start date is the previous April 1, meaning that on and shortly after April 1, employers begin filing petitions with a postdated October 1 start date.

### Exceptions to the Cap

There are exceptions to the 65,000 cap amount. For 2012, an additional 20,000 H-1B visas have been set aside for U.S. master's degree holders. And as a result of the Free Trade Act,

## Advice of Counsel

In fiscal year 2011, 58,200 H-1B standard cap numbers were available. Of the 6,800 that were reserved for Singapore and Chilean nationals, fewer than 800 were used, so they were rereleased into the cap, making the aggregate 64,271. There were also 20,000 petitions against the 20,000-cap exemption for foreign nationals holding U.S. advanced degrees. As a result of the global economic downturn that begin in the summer of 2008, the cap was less of a problem to employers in early 2011 given the fewer number of H-1B applicants. That being said, the cap for fiscal 2011 was hit on January 26, 2011—less than four months after the fiscal year began.

6,800 H-1B visas have been set aside for workers from Singapore and Chile. H-1B employees hired by institutions of higher learning, affiliated research organizations, nonprofit research organizations, and governmental research organizations are also exempt from the cap.

# Portability

H-1B employees are allowed to transfer their H-1B status to another employer, a concept known as portability. By contrast, other visa holders must first obtain an approved change or amendment of status petition before they can begin work for a new employer. H-1B

## Visa Vocab

*Portability* means that foreigners with H-1B visas may begin working for a new employer with their H-1B visas when they file the petition with USCIS; the H-1B status is portable to the new employer. Again, this only applies to transfers of an H-1B visa from (old) Employer X to (new) Employer Y.

workers, however, may begin work immediately after their new H-1B case for the new employer is filed, provided the case is nonfrivolous and they are in status when the petition is filed.

As you can imagine, the doctrine of portability gives foreign nationals with H-1B visas great flexibility. They can switch jobs with a high degree of confidence regarding their visa status, whereas other NIV holders must first have their case approved before they can switch jobs.

## Why the Complexity?

Why does the H-1B visa permit the portability doctrine, but other NIVs do not?

The reason is that historically, the H-1B visa has been the political football of the visa world, and consequently rules and exceptions to rules have grown around it like barnacles. Large companies have aggressively lobbied for its use, while labor organizations denounce the visa as a tool for companies to exploit cheaper foreign labor. Over the last dozen years, labor organizations and their Democratic Party allies have sought to impose restrictions on its use (such as the LCA requirements, the cap, and so forth), while business and its Republican Party allies have tried to liberalize its use by increasing the cap and creating the portability doctrine to give employers more hiring flexibility.

In short, the regulations regarding the H-1B visa have been drafted by a number of competing agencies and interests, and, therefore, like the camel drawn up by the horse committee, the H-1B visa is both a durable animal and a bit of an ugly and ungainly mess.

That being said, it remains perhaps the best known and most common employment NIV, certainly for those with advanced degrees.

CHAPTER 9

# The L-1A and L-1B Visas

## In This Chapter

➤ Transferring employees to the United States

➤ Which companies qualify

➤ Managers and executives

➤ Those with specialized knowledge

The L-1 visa was created for professionals of multinational corporations so they could work abroad for a company that has a U.S. office or presence. It allows professional-level employees to bring their skills and knowledge to the United States while working for the same company.

## The Intracompany Transferee Visa

The L-1 visa is the vehicle of choice to transfer those employees to the United States in certain executive or specialized capacities. It is flexible, relatively straightforward, and (thanks to the doctrine of dual intent) can be used as a springboard for eventually obtaining a green card. All in all, for those who qualify the L-1 is the visa of choice. Not that it is easy to qualify for one. The L-1 visa is reserved for multinational managers and executives or others with specialized knowledge.

### Basic Requirements for the L-1 Visa

The basic requirements for eligibility for the L-1 visa are as follows:

➤ The applicant is transferring between offices of the same company, from one abroad to one in the United States (hence the term *intracompany transferees*).

➤ The applicant has worked abroad for the overseas company for at least one year out of the last three years.

➤ The applicant has worked abroad and is being transferred to the United States in an executive or managerial function or has specialized knowledge of the company.

Although seemingly straightforward, there is a great deal of nuance in the above requirements.

### A and B

The L-1 visa comes in two flavors: A and B. The L-1A visa is for multinational managers or executives, and the L-1B visa is for those who have specialized knowledge.

Initial admission to the United States for L-1 visa holders (except those entering the United States to be employed at a new office, discussed below) is for a maximum period of three years. Extensions of stay in increments of two years may be granted. L-1A managers and executives may remain in the United States in L-1A status for up to seven years. L-1B specialized knowledge employees may remain in the United States in L-1 status for up to five years. Spouses and minor children are entitled to remain in the United States for the same period as the principal.

Those are the basics. Now, how do you qualify?

# Qualifying Organizations—How the Foreign and U.S. Companies Relate

The first step in demonstrating eligibility for the L-1 visa is to show that the overseas company (for whom the applicant works) and the U.S. entity (to which he or she is being transferred) are related, or in immigration jargon are qualifying organizations.

### Visa Vocab

A qualifying organization means that the overseas employer and the U.S. company have a permitted, or qualifying, relationship between them for L visa eligibility purposes.

## Relationships Between the Companies

Generally, four types of relationships are recognized as qualifying for L-1 purposes:

> ➤ Parent/Subsidiary: the U.S. company owns 51 percent or more of the foreign company (or vice versa)

> ➤ Affiliate: 51 percent or more of both companies is owned by a common parent company

> ➤ Joint venture: U.S. entities are owned equally by two parent companies

> ➤ Branch office: the foreign company has established an office in the United States but has not necessarily established a formal legal entity (or vice versa)

In cases where a large publicly traded multinational organization has a wholly owned foreign subsidiary, proving a qualifying relationship between the two should be relatively easy. Other cases however are not as clear.

### Example Please

In some cases, demonstrating the qualifying relationship between companies is not difficult. For instance, if an applicant works for a large British PLC and is being transferred to the British PLC's wholly owned U.S. subsidiary, the link is obvious: parent/subsidiary. Similarly, a clear-cut link can be seen between a large Japanese conglomerate with wholly owned subsidiaries in both France (where the applicant works) and the United States (where he or she is being transferred): the two companies are affiliates by virtue of their common ownership by the Japanese parent company.

## Joint Ventures

Suppose an applicant is being transferred to work for an American company that is 50-percent owned by a British PLC and 50-percent owned by a French PLC. This company doesn't qualify as a subsidiary or affiliate because for L-1 visa purposes, 51 percent of the company must be owned by the related company. In this case, each parent company owns 50 percent of the U.S. company, so it's technically neither a subsidiary nor an affiliate of the foreign parent, but a joint venture.

The regulations make a specific exception for joint ventures. The rules provide that a company owned equally by two parent companies is a subsidiary of both parent companies (for L-1 visa purposes), so either parent company, even though they each own only 50 percent of the joint venture, may transfer employees to the joint venture company.

What about a U.S. joint venture that is owned equally (33 percent) by three parent companies?

In some cases, the parent company can own even less than 50 percent of the U.S. company and still qualify, provided it can demonstrate that it has governing control over the U.S. company. This is obviously more difficult to prove than the straightforward subsidiary or joint venture examples. After all, proving ownership is pretty straightforward; proving control is more difficult.

## Branch Offices

Finally, branch offices are also technically eligible for qualifying for L-1 purposes. Like joint ventures, branch offices can be problematic in that there may not be a formal entity (such as a corporation) to point to. Because there is no formal entity, amassing the evidence to show that a branch office exists may be challenging. Similarly, branch offices are in many cases smaller operations, and therefore the government may look at these cases with more scrutiny than, say, a formal subsidiary.

By the same token, it can be difficult to prove that there is a qualifying relationship between some associated organizations such as nonprofit corporations, schools, or hospitals because no one actually owns the company.

## How to Prove the Qualifying Relationship

Even cases that should be open-and-shut (such as the instance where a foreign entity wholly owns a U.S. subsidiary) can sometimes be challenging to document. Large companies often have complex and convoluted ownership structures, with multiple levels of ownership or dozens of intermediary holding companies between the parent (at the top) and the subsidiary (at the bottom) of the organizational structure.

In all but the most clear-cut corporate relationships of parent and subsidiary companies, stock certificates, affidavits, and organizational charts may have to be produced (or created) to prove the link between the companies. Establishing the qualifying relationship through transparent, crystal-clear documentation often requires a great deal of detective work but is essential in getting the L visa approved.

## One-Year-Abroad Requirement

Assuming you can establish that a qualifying relationship exists, the next step is to prove that the transferee was employed in a managerial, executive, or specialized knowledge capacity by an overseas entity for at least one year of the preceding three years prior to the transfer. Any time spent in the United States during this period does not count toward the one year spent abroad.

### Advice of Counsel

The L visa requires the applicant to have worked for an overseas company for one year in the past three. That one year does not have to be the immediately preceding year, though; any twelve-month period during the previous three years suffices, even if the individual left employment at the foreign company and then returned. It doesn't have to be one continuous year of employment either. An aggregate of twelve months can be compiled during the three-year period.

The seemingly straightforward one-year-abroad requirement can, however, create headaches. For example, if the individual has spent considerable time in the United States over the past three years, say traveling in and out on a B visa, he or she will have to compile a record of time abroad to make sure that a total of one year abroad can be proven. Sometimes, a month-by-month chronicle of time spent abroad vs. time spent in the United States is required, particularly if the individual has worked for the company for just a year or so.

## L-1A: Executives and Managers

The next step is showing that the applicant's job qualifies. Individuals serving as executives or managers abroad may be eligible for the L-1A visa to fulfill similar duties in the United States. Note that the exact duties do not have to be the same in both roles. The CEO of a British PLC can be transferred as an L-1A to serve as the CFO of the British PLC's U.S. subsidiary—both (CEO and CFO) are executive duties. In cases where the most senior managers of the company are involved, such as the CEO or CFO, it should be relatively straightforward to show that the job at issue is managerial or executive.

But what about instances where a company is very small? Suppose the foreign company has only ten employees, and its president is being transferred to the U.S. subsidiary to act as its sole employee in the role of CEO. Sure, the title is executive—but what does that mean if a company has only one employee? Similarly, many international banks have thousands of employees whose job title is vice president. Is that considered a managerial role? Well, it depends.

## *Executives Defined*

In the view of the immigration service, an executive role is one in which the employee

> ➤ primarily directs the management or a major component or function of the organization;

> ➤ establishes goals and policies;

> ➤ exercises wide latitude in discretionary decision making; and

> ➤ receives only general supervision from higher-level executives, such as the board of directors or the stockholders.

An executive normally has other senior level officials reporting to him or her, although the number of such subordinates is not dispositive. For example, the CFO of a company is considered to be an executive because he manages the financial function of the company. This is true whether or not the executive has many (or any) direct reports. A vice president with limited job responsibilities somewhere in middle management, however, may or may not qualify. The clear intention behind the executive category is that the individual be at or near the top of the corporate ladder.

An individual who is not at or near the top of the corporate ladder, however, might still qualify as a manager, the other slot into which a job can fit and still qualify for an L-1A.

## *Managers Defined*

Simply managing other people does not make someone a manager in the eyes of immigration authorities. For example, a manager of a manufacturing line supervising a dozen unskilled or semiskilled workers generally does not qualify as a manager for L-1A purposes; nor would a foreman of a construction project, irrespective of how many people he or she supervises. For L-1A purposes, the individuals managed should also be professional in nature (such as an HR manager or accounting manager being managed by the COO).

So then, what makes a manager? In the eyes of the immigration authorities, a manager is one who primarily

> ➤ manages the organization or a department, subdivision, function, or component of a company;

> ➤ supervises and controls the work of other supervisory, professional, or managerial employees, or manages an essential function within the organization, department, or subdivision;

➤ has the authority to hire and fire or recommend personnel actions if directly supervising employees, or if not supervising employees serves on a senior level within the organization with respect to the function managed; and

➤ exercises discretion over the day-to-day operations of the activity or function.

The important word in the above definition is *and* because the immigration authorities, at least in marginal cases, scrutinize every one of the four elements above to see whether the employee at issue meets all of these requirements.

Suffice it to say that proving a particular role is executive or managerial requires an explanation and characterization of the job's functions in light of the expectations set forth above, including evidence, particularly of those managed and what they do, such as a job description or an organizational chart.

# L-1B: Specialized Knowledge

For individuals who do not qualify for the L-1A route, a second category exists for employees with specialized knowledge. What constitutes specialized knowledge in the view of the government is knowledge of a company's "product, service, research, equipment, techniques, management, or other interests and its application in international markets, or an advanced level of knowledge or expertise in the organization's processes and procedures."

## *Specialized Knowledge Further Defined*

The immigration service has offered additional criteria to determine what is or is not sufficiently specialized.

➤ Knowledge that is valuable to the employer's competitiveness in the marketplace

➤ Unique qualifications to contribute to the U.S. employer's knowledge of foreign operating conditions

➤ Knowledge that stems from a key employee being utilized abroad and given significant assignments that have enhanced the employer's productivity, competitiveness, image, or financial position

➤ Knowledge that can only be gained through extensive prior experience with that employer

**Visa Vocab**

Having specialized knowledge means having knowledge that is unique to the company or its products that can only be acquired through experience in the company

Specialized knowledge is knowledge that is not widely known, even within the company itself. Information that is generally known within the industry (how to make steel, for example) does not qualify. However, knowledge of how to make a unique, proprietary type of commercially valuable steel might qualify.

As you can imagine, what constitutes specialized knowledge is pretty subjective. Not surprisingly, a great number of L-1B visa applications get hung up on trying to prove whether an individual has such knowledge or not.

If this category sounds like a bit of a crap shoot to you, you are not alone. Specialized knowledge is quite similar to the Supreme Court's definition of pornography: it's hard to define, but you know it when you see it. For that reason, an L-1B visa is sometimes only as good as the attorney who prepared it.

# New Office Petitions

A final issue arises when the U.S. entity (parent, subsidiary, branch office, or affiliate) has been doing business in the United States for less than one year. These are called new office L-1 petitions. New office petitions are essentially the same as regular L-1 petitions except they require additional evidentiary burdens, and they are approved only for the initial one-year period (rather than three).

In new office L-1 petitions, the company must demonstrate it has sufficient physical premises and that the intended U.S. operation is of sufficient size to support an executive or managerial position by providing information regarding:

> ➤ the nature and scope of the proposed U.S. office, its organizational structure, and financial goals;

> ➤ the size of the U.S. investment and financial ability of the foreign company to pay the employees and commence doing business; and

> ➤ the organizational structure of the foreign entity.

Large foreign companies making sizeable investments in the United States generally do not have a difficult time meeting the new office requirements. However, for small companies with only a few U.S. employees, proving to the government's satisfaction that the U.S. enterprise has the wherewithal to do business can be something of a challenge.

## *Beyond the First Year*

After the initial one-year period, the company must show that its U.S. business is operating and has grown enough to support an executive or manager. Failure to show an increase in factors such as gross income and staffing levels may result in a denial of the extension request. No company wants to send an executive overseas for one year with the threat that at the end of the first year he or she will be unable to get a visa renewal. For these reasons, new office petitions can be an administrative hassle and burden for small start-ups.

# Blanket Petitions

Some large multinational corporations qualify for what is called an L-1 blanket. The L-1 blanket allows a large company to prequalify for the transfer of its L-1 employees. Once the L-1 blanket is approved, the company may transfer executive/managerial and specialized knowledge employees to the United States on L-1 visas without having to file a separate petition for each employee with USCIS. Instead, each applicant applies directly at the consulate, where a consular officer will examine the substantive eligibility of each applicant and whether the job at issue qualifies. This process can make marginal cases somewhat more difficult.

### Visa Vocab

A blanket petition is an approval notice for a specific company that allows any of its employees to apply at a consulate for an L-1 visa. This keeps the USCIS from having to adjudicate dozens of L-1 cases that have the same qualifying relationship at issue, as is the case with many large multinational companies. It allows the consuls to simply focus on the bona fides of the individual applicant and job.

## Blanket Requirements

A company may qualify for an L-1 blanket if it meets one or more of the following requirements:

➤ The U.S. company has at least 1,000 employees

➤ The U.S. company has obtained L-1 visas for at least ten of its employees during the previous twelve months

➤ The U.S. company and related U.S. companies have a combined annual sales of at least $25 million.

A blanket petition is initially issued for three years. Provided the company still meets the requirements after those three years, the renewal of the blanket petition can be requested for indefinite approval. Once a blanket petition is approved, the company's employees are eligible to go directly to the U.S. consulate in their home country to apply for a visa to enter the United States. They must prove to the consul that they qualify as a manager, executive, or employee with specialized knowledge. The blanket is a streamlined method for a foreign employer to bring in many L-1 applicants with less paperwork and hassle.

# How to Apply for an L Visa

The U.S. employer normally files the initial L-1 petition with the appropriate USCIS service center in the United States. The only exception to this filing procedure is for Canadian citizens, who may file a petition at the same time they apply for admission to the United States at a class A port of entry.

**Visa Vocab**

A class A port of entry is a port where any foreign national may apply for entry to the United States.

Once approval is granted by USCIS, the transferring employee, his or her spouse and minor children (under the age of twenty-one) apply for L-1 and L-2 visas, respectively, at a U.S. consulate. Spouses and children admitted to the United States under L-2 visas are not authorized to work in the United States, but spouses may apply for employment authorization upon arrival, which is generally granted approximately three months after the application is filed. Again, Canadian citizens are visa-exempt and are not required to apply for visas at a U.S. consulate.

CHAPTER 10

# The E-1 Treaty Trader and E-2 Treaty Investor Visas

## In This Chapter

> ➤ Visas made by treaties
> ➤ E visas are country specific
> ➤ E-1 is for trade
> ➤ E-2 is for investment

Investment and trade are the keys to international commerce. And thankfully there is a nonimmigrant visa category designed for certain foreign nationals whose companies engage in substantial trade with or make a substantial investment in the United States. These are the two E visa categories: the E-1 treaty trader visa and the E-2 treaty investor visa.

## Step 1: Is There a Treaty?

Note that the word *treaty* occurs in the name of both visas. This is not an accident, and it underscores an important and unique fact about the E visas. Unlike all other employment-related nonimmigrants visas, which were created by Congress, E visas were created by various international treaties between the United States and certain foreign countries.

Put in simple terms, certain foreign countries offer an E-1 trade treaty or an E-2 investment treaty with

**Visa Vocab**

E-1 visas are for foreign companies trading with the United States; E-2 visas are for foreign companies investing in the United States.

the United States; some countries offer both and some offer neither. For example, Albania offers an E-2 but not an E-1 treaty with the United States. Honduras offers both an E-1 and an E-2 treaty with the United States. This is true of most Western European countries. The People's Republic of China does not have either treaty, so the E visa is not available to any citizens of the PRC.

## No USCIS Approval Required

Because E visas are the creatures of treaties, there is another side effect. Treaties are the province of the Department of State. The DOS also runs the consular section of U.S. embassies, which is the division that issues visas. Therefore, U.S. consuls have the ability to adjudicate and issue E visas directly—without any preapproval from USCIS.

As we saw in chapter 4, most nonimmigrant visas require preapproval from USCIS via the I-797 approval notice form. That is not the case with E visas.

With an E visa, just as with a B visa, you can skip the petition entirely and apply directly at an embassy. Is that a good thing? Well, it depends. The filings are done at a consulate, and each has its own rules and regulations that need to be followed, which takes a bit of research on your part. And although it cuts out a step in the process, the process may take longer because the consular officials are not simply relying on an earlier approval, they are adjudicating the case themselves. Also, a consul takes a much harder and more thoughtful assessment of a case than a USCIS official does in most situations. If the case is marginal, you may have problems.

### Advice of Counsel

You are permitted to file an E petition with USCIS, but a USCIS petition approval carries little or no weight in the DOS's decision to issue a visa. DOS makes its own review regardless of what USCIS recommends—remember, the DOS, not USCIS, issues visas.

But USCIS has jurisdiction over an individual's status while in the United States. So people who enter the United States with an E visa issued by DOS may file petitions with USCIS to extend their status without dealing with the DOS at all if they have remained in the United States and do not need to leave and obtain a new visa.

# Step 2: Determining Nationality

The E visa is country specific; only nationals of countries that have particular treaties with the United States are eligible. But nationals of the treaty country at issue must own at least 50 percent of the U.S. entity involved.

Let's assume a French company wishes to transfer an employee to work at its subsidiary in the United States. French nationals own 100 percent of this French company as well as 100 percent of the U.S. subsidiary. France offers both an E-1 and E-2 treaty with the United States. Assuming the individuals otherwise qualify, the French company could send over French managerial types to the U.S. subsidiary with either an E-1 or E-2 visa. But they could send only French nationals; no other nationals (British, German, etc.) would be eligible.

Further assume the company was publicly traded on the Paris Stock Exchange. In that case, the French company still qualifies. The nationality of the parent public company is presumed to be that of the country in which its stock is listed. So a company publicly listed on the Paris Stock Exchange is deemed to be French, a company listed in Frankfurt is deemed to be German, and so forth.

What if a French national who is living and working in the United States as an E visa holder owns 51 percent of the U.S. company? That's fine—in fact, the E visa is widely used by owners of U.S. businesses so they can oversee or inspect their U.S. investment.

## Losing Nationality for E Purposes

Nationality, however, like car keys, is easily lost. To continue with the example above, if the French national who owns 51 percent of a business were to sell all of his or her shares to a German investor, the company would no longer be considered a French entity and any French E visa holders would be out of status (and out of luck). But the company could be eligible for German E visa status.

Or if the French owner receives lawful permanent residency and a green card, he or she is not deemed eligible for E status. Once the majority owner is a permanent U.S. resident, the company's E status disappears—in an instant.

This is more than a theoretical problem in the world of international business. A large company could have hundreds of managers and executives in the United States pursuant to a particular E visa status. E visa holders of a company that is bought by another company deemed to be of a different nationality would be immediately impacted.

# The E-1 Treaty Trader Visa

Two E visa categories are available to companies depending on the nature of their business.

One is the E-1 treaty trader visa. This visa applies to companies principally engaged in substantial international trade between the United States and the E treaty country. The exact type of trade generally does not matter. The trade can be in goods or services; widgets or financial products; tourism or engineering.

What does matter is that the trade be principally between the United States and the treaty country, and that the volume of trade is substantial.

### Visa Vocab

*Principally* in this case refers to the requirement that more than 50 percent of a foreign company's international trade be with the United States. Put differently, the volume of trade between the United States and the treaty country must account for more than 50 percent of the U.S. company's trading revenues.

## *Trade Must Be Substantial*

*Substantial* is a term used for both the E-1 and E-2 visa. In the E-1 context, *substantial* is defined as "an amount of trade sufficient to ensure a continuous flow of trade." A single transaction is not enough, even if it is very large. What the government wants to see is an ongoing pattern of trade.

What is the dollar value of substantial trade? There is no minimum threshold. Generally, the government looks for income proportional to the type and size of the industry. What matters to the government is not so much value as volume. The type of evidence needed to satisfy the volume of trade includes commercial invoices, bills of sale, customer receipts, trade brochures, and the like.

Except for pure trading enterprises, such as brokerages, the requirement that the trade be principally between the United States and the treaty country, coupled with the amorphous substantial value of trade requirement, the E-1 category is somewhat less appealing (and harder to document) than its sister category, the E-2. Most U.S. businesses that would qualify for the E-1 would qualify for the E-2 category as well, and in our experience the documentary requirements of the E-2 visa are somewhat easier to prove. With that in mind, we turn to the E-2 visa.

# The E-2 Investment Visa

The E-2 visa applies to businesses that make a substantial investment in the United States. The first question always asked is, how much is substantial?

## Substantial Investment

There is no monetary threshold that defines whether an investment is substantial for E-2 purposes. We have seen instances where investments of $50,000 have qualified and $250,000 have been challenged. One rule of thumb is that the investment must be proportional to the type and nature of the business. The intention is not to discriminate against small or start-up businesses. The government recognizes that some types of businesses—service businesses, for example—might by their very nature need less capital. Small investments should not be disqualified if the level of investment is appropriate for the type of business. That being said, the more invested and more tangible and substantive the business, the better the case.

### Advice of Counsel

One general guideline for small- and medium-sized businesses is to plan to invest at least half the value of the business or the usual amount required to start up a similar business. Investment funds may be borrowed so long as the investor (and not just the U.S. subsidiary) is liable for the debt.

## Proportionality Test

In addition, the size of the investment is assessed by how proportional it is to the percentage of its foreign ownership. This is called the proportionality test. The foreign national or parent company that owns a lower percentage of the company makes a bigger investment.

Let's say an Australian company is investing $200,000 in an American widget-making business. If the Australian company owns 60 percent of the U.S. business, the amount of the investment ($200,000) might be considered substantial. If, on the other hand, the Australian company owns 100 percent, then the amount might not. The investment amount will be judged proportionally to how much the foreign company owns. Again, there is no mathematical formula or rule as to what percentage a company must own vs. how much it must invest. Each case is assessed on its own merits. Suffice it to say, however, that the greater the investment and the greater the percentage of ownership, the better the chances of approval.

## Other Investment Factors

In addition to the requirement that the investment be substantial, there are specific guidelines regarding the nature of the investment.

> ➤ The investment must be at risk; the government wants to see that the investment is subject to loss if the business fails. Why? Because it wants to see that the investment is real and that the investor (be it a company or an individual) has some skin in the game. For that reason, inheriting a business in the United States would not qualify as an investment.

> ➤ The investment must be entrepreneurial—not passive. Merely owning stocks or real estate in the United States would not qualify. The business has to be active, operating, and profit focused. Nonprofit companies do not qualify for E-2 status.

> ➤ The investment must not be marginal, meaning the investment must have the possibility to expand, grow, and create more jobs. The purpose of the investment must be to generate other job opportunities, preferably with good, high-wage jobs. A business that generates sufficient income only for the owner and his family is considered marginal.

## E Visas for the Majority Owner of the Business

Assuming the above qualifications are met, the next issue is whether the individual qualifies for an E-2 visa. In many cases, the U.S. business is small or medium in size and privately owned by the foreign national—either directly, meaning he or she owns the U.S. company, or indirectly, meaning he or she is the ultimate or majority owner of a foreign company that in turn owns 50 percent or more of the U.S. entity.

The owner of an E-2 business qualifies in most cases for an E-2 visa if the job requires him or her to develop and direct the U.S. business. In addition, the individual must exercise control over the company. Control may be shown by ownership (51 percent or more) or by operational control, such as control over the board of directors, stock or voting agreements, or other contracts. Obviously, the easiest way to show the ability to direct and control the business is through pure majority ownership, but control can be demonstrated in other ways if the ownership is, say, 50 percent. Negative control in the cases of 50/50 joint ventures—meaning the power of the owner to block certain corporate actions, usually through shareholder agreements and supermajority rights—also suffice to show control.

The government wants to see that the individual is involved in some capacity as a hands-on owner, not just as a passive stockholder. Mere ownership of the company is not enough, however. After all, the purpose of the visa is for the individual to manage the company, not to give that individual and his or her family a free pass to enter the United States simply because he or she happens to own a business.

As a practical matter, proving that the majority owner qualifies is rarely a problem, given that the company has given him or her an appropriate title and duties—he or she is, after all, the owner.

## E Visas for Other Executives and Supervisors

The above requirements only apply in the case of the owner of an E-2 business seeking an E-2 visa. Other individuals are eligible for an E-2 visa as employees, provided they are serving in the United States in an executive, supervisory, or essential skills function.

### Advice of Counsel

You may have noticed that these categories sound suspiciously like the qualifications for L-1A (managers or executives) or L-1B (specialized knowledge) that we discussed in chapter 9. While the categories are not exactly the same, there is no denying that they broadly overlap in most respects, and any case that would make a good L-1A case will almost certainly make a good E case. The same goes with any good L-1B case.

For executives and supervisors seeking E status, the U.S. job duties must prove that the employee has ultimate control and responsibility for the business's overall operation (as with a chief operating officer) or a major function of it (as with a controller)—just as with the L-1A. However, the criteria making the assessment are slightly different.

Criteria the government looks at for deciding whether a position is executive or supervisory are as follows:

➤ The executive position provides great authority to determine policy and direction

➤ The supervisory position provides supervision for a significant portion of the company and involves high-level employees

➤ The applicant possesses executive/supervisory skills and experience

➤ The job title and salary are commensurate for this type role

➤ The applicant holds a high position in the company's organizational chart

➤ The applicant is responsible for making discretionary decisions, setting policies, directing and managing business operations, or supervising other professional level employees

➤ Any routine staff work required is only ancillary

As you can see, a totality of factors is involved in showing the job function is executive in nature. How does one prove this? By showing the U.S. job description, the foreign job description, the applicant's resume, an organizational chart, a letter from the company, and similar documents. No single factor—job title, for example—will suffice. A job that is designated as senior executive assistant but pays $21,000 a year with principal responsibilities that include fetching coffee will not qualify, even if the individual reports directly to the CEO.

## Essential Workers

The above individual might qualify, however, in the other broad E category—that of being an essential worker. The essential worker category is obviously different from the L-1B specialized knowledge category, although in reality one of the best ways to prove that someone is essential is in fact by showing that he or she has specialized knowledge or similar attributes. The factors the government will consider in this respect include:

> ➤ The individual's degree or proven expertise in the area of operations
> ➤ The individual's uniqueness of specific skills
> ➤ The function the individual will fill
> ➤ The salary the position carries
> ➤ The availability of U.S. workers for the position

Obviously—as with the L-1B category of specialized knowledge—whether an employee is essential can be pretty subjective. In one sense, the fact that a foreign company wants to go through the time and effort to get the person a visa should attest to the fact that the company believes he or she is essential—but of course nothing is so simple. It still needs to be proved to Uncle Sam.

Usually this proof comes in the form of a testamentary letter from the company, often drafted by the company's immigration counsel hitting all of the above hot buttons). Other evidence, such as organizational charts, position descriptions, and the like, are generally necessary as well. The individual's skills do not have to be unique, but rather, in the words of the government, they need to be "indispensible to the success of the business."

Finally, as a reminder, any E employee must of course be of the same nationality as the E company, irrespective of the nature of the job.

## How to Apply

As mentioned above, the E visa falls squarely within the jurisdiction of the DOS. Therefore, applications are generally made directly to the applicable consulate (French consulate for French applicants), without filing for an approved petition from USCIS.

The consul usually looks at the application in two parts: First, the underlying corporate eligibility for the company to have E status—meaning, is it engaged in substantial trade or has it made a substantial investment? This is the hardest and most time-consuming part of the application. Second, the initial applicant and any subsequent applicants are reviewed to see if they individually qualify, irrespective of whether the company qualifies. To put it differently, the consul might determine that a company is E eligible because it made a substantial investment, but the individual is not because the consul doesn't believe he or she is a manager.

Once the company is qualified, proving the bona fides of the company and the nature of the investment is usually not required again, although a consul may request a company to update its information every few years to confirm it remains eligible.

Both the applicant and his or her family are given E-2 visas, which are good for periods of between two and five years, depending on which consulate in which country issues them. Spouses of individuals with E visas are eligible to apply for work permission once they enter the United States.

# CHAPTER 11

# The O and P Visas for those with Extraordinary Abilities

## In This Chapter

➤ The four categories of the O visa

➤ Extraordinary ability and the evidentiary criteria

➤ How to apply for an O visa

➤ The P visa for athletes and group entertainers

➤ Internationally recognized and some exceptions

➤ The P-1 visa process

Thus far we have discussed visas for tourists and business visitors, which include managers and executives of businesses. But what about visas for the truly exceptional among us?

Suppose you are world famous in your area of expertise like international soccer star David Beckham or British theoretical physicist Stephen Hawking—what kind of visa might you be eligible for?

Somewhat counterintuitively, you probably would not be eligible for the most common employment visas such as the H1-B (professional worker). After all, if you are Beckham you don't have a professional degree in your area of expertise, which is required for the H-1B, and your position (professional soccer player) doesn't require an advanced degree—even if you were captain of the English national team. And although Dr. Hawking pretty clearly would make it over the advanced degree-holder requirement of the H-1B, what happens when the annual cap has already been met and there are no H-1B visas available?

The O-1 visa is for the individual who possesses extraordinary ability in the sciences, arts, education, business, or athletics. The P-1 visa is for the athlete who performs at a specific event as part of a group or team that is internationally recognized, or a person who performs with or is an integral or essential part of an entertainment group that has been recognized internationally.

### Advice of Counsel

O visas are generally used by individuals and fit situations where they may be in the United States for extended periods. P visas are generally used by group artists who are in the United States for briefer periods. The distinction can be fuzzy, though, so you may want to consult an attorney to determine which of these visas are best suited for your purposes.

# The O Visa

The O visa comes in four categories.

➤ The O-1A visa is for individuals with an extraordinary ability in the sciences, education, business, or athletics, not including those in the arts or in the motion picture or television industries.

➤ The O-1B visa is for individuals with an extraordinary ability in the arts or extraordinary achievement in the motion picture or television industries.

➤ The O-2 visa is available for individuals such as backup singers/musicians and technical crew who accompany an O-1 artist or athlete to assist in a specific event or performance. To qualify for the O-2 visa, the individual's assistance must be an integral part of the O-1 visa holder's activity, and he or she must have critical skills and experience with the O-1 that cannot be readily performed by a U.S. worker.

➤ The O-3 visa exists for the spouse or children of O-1 and O-2 visa holders.

## Extraordinary Ability Defined

What is extraordinary ability, and how do you prove you have it?

To qualify for an O-1 visa, the beneficiary must demonstrate extraordinary ability by sustained national or international acclaim and must be traveling to the United States to continue work in the area of extraordinary ability on a temporary basis.

### Visa Vocab

The term *extraordinary ability* generally refers to those who have risen to the very top of their professions.

Specifically, for O-1A applicants in the fields of science, education, business, or athletics, *extraordinary ability* is defined as a level of expertise indicating that the person is one of a small percentage who has risen to the very top of the field of endeavor.

For O-1B artists, *extraordinary ability* is defined as reaching a high level of achievement in a specific artistic field evidenced by a degree of skill and recognition that is substantially above what is ordinarily encountered to the extent that a person described as prominent is renowned, leading, or well known in the field.

## How to Prove You are Extraordinary

To qualify for an O-1A (sciences, education, business, or athletics) visa, the beneficiary must show evidence that he or she has received a major internationally recognized award such as a Nobel Prize or evidence of at least three of the following:

➤ Receipt of nationally or internationally recognized prizes or awards for excellence in the field of endeavor

➤ Membership in associations in the field for which classification is sought that requires outstanding achievements as judged by recognized national or international experts in the field

➤ Published material in professional or major trade publications, newspapers, or other major media about the beneficiary and the beneficiary's work in the field for which classification is being sought

➤ Original scientific, scholarly, or business-related contributions of major significance in the field

➤ Authorship of scholarly articles in professional journals or other major media in the field for which classification is being sought

➤ A high salary or other remuneration for services as evidenced by contracts or other reliable evidence

> ➤ Participation on a panel or individually as a judge of the work of others in the same or in a field of specialization allied to that field for which classification is being sought

> ➤ Employment in a critical or essential capacity for organizations and establishments that have a distinguished reputation

If the above standards do not readily apply to the beneficiary's occupation, he or she may submit comparable evidence in order to establish eligibility.

### Advice of Counsel

Unlike specialized knowledge as in the L-1B visa category or other terms that are inherently subjective, the O visa category is quite specific as to what kinds of evidence must be provided to meet the definition of extraordinary. Of course, there is still some degree of subjectivity involved. For example, when is a scientific contribution considered being of major significance, as opposed to minor significance, in the field?

To qualify for the O-1B (arts) visa, the beneficiary must show evidence that he or she has received or has been nominated for a significant national or international award or prize in the particular field, such as an Academy Award, Emmy, or Grammy Award; or evidence of at least three of the following:

> ➤ Has performed or will perform services as a lead or starring participant in productions or events that have a distinguished reputation as evidenced by critical reviews, advertisements, publicity releases, publications, contracts, or endorsements

> ➤ National or international recognition for achievements as shown by critical reviews or other published materials by or about the beneficiary in major newspapers, trade journals, magazines, or other publications

> ➤ Has performed or will perform in a lead, starring, or critical role for organizations and establishments that have a distinguished reputation as evidenced by articles in newspapers, trade journals, publications, or testimonials

> ➤ A record of major commercial or critically acclaimed successes as shown by such indicators as title, rating, or standing in the field; box office receipts; motion picture or television ratings; and other occupational achievements reported in trade journals, major newspapers, or other publications

➤ Received significant recognition for achievements from organizations, critics, government agencies, or other recognized experts in the field in which the beneficiary is engaged, with the testimonials clearly indicating the expert's authority, expertise, and knowledge of the beneficiary's achievements.

➤ A high salary or other substantial remuneration for services in relation to others in the field as shown by contracts or other reliable evidence.

➤ If the above standards do not readily apply to the beneficiary's occupation in the arts, he or she may submit comparable evidence in order to establish eligibility (this exception does not apply to the motion picture or television industry).

## The O-1 Petition Process

To apply for an O visa, the petitioner needs to file form I-129 with the appropriate USCIS service center.

An interesting distinction made with the O visa (and the P visa explained below) is who may serve as the petitioner. Typically with employment-based visas, the U.S. company for whom the beneficiary will work serves as the petitioner. However, with O and P visas, particularly in the arts, a petitioner may be someone else, such as the beneficiary's representing U.S. agent; a representative of both the employer and the beneficiary; or a person or entity authorized by the employer to act for or in place of the employer as its agent.

A petitioner who files as an agent for multiple employers (for example, an agent who represents a musician recording for two labels) must establish that he or she is duly authorized to act as an agent for the other employers. Agents filing I-129 petitions for multiple employers must include with the petition:

➤ Supporting documentation, including a complete itinerary of the event or events, that specifies the dates of each service or engagement, the names and addresses of the actual employers, and the names and addresses of the establishments, venues, or locations where the services will be performed

➤ Contracts between the agent and the employers

➤ Contracts between the actual employers and the beneficiary

➤ An explanation of the terms and conditions of the employment accompanied by the required documentation

## The O-1 Filing Requirements

Once the petitioner is determined, the I-129 form should be filed (no more than one year before the actual need for the beneficiary's services) with documentary evidence that includes the required consultation, contract between petitioner and beneficiary, itinerary and/or petitioner letter, and evidence that the beneficiary meets the regulatory criteria.

The required consultation must be in the form of a written advisory opinion from a peer group (including labor organizations) or a person designated by the group with expertise in the beneficiary's area of ability. If the O-1 petition is for an individual with extraordinary achievement in motion pictures or television, a consultation must come from an appropriate labor union and a management organization with expertise in the beneficiary's area of ability.

There are exceptions to the consultation requirement. If the petitioner can demonstrate that an appropriate peer group, including a labor organization, does not exist, the decision will be based on the evidence of record.

A consultation may also be waived in the field of arts if the beneficiary seeks readmission on an O-1B visa to perform similar services within two years of the date of a previous consultation. Petitioners should submit a waiver request and a copy of the previous consultation with the petition.

### Example Please

A French film producer applying for an O-1B visa would be required to obtain a consultation from both an appropriate labor union (such as the Producers Guild of America) and a management organization (such as Alliance of Motion Picture and TV Producers) because within the entertainment industry, these organizations are common. However a Nobel Prize–winning Chinese biochemist applying for an O-1A to perform research with a renowned cancer institute would likely not have an appropriate peer group/labor organization from which to obtain a consultation.

A copy of any written contract between the petitioner and the beneficiary, or a summary of the terms of the contract under which the beneficiary will be employed should be included in the petition filing. USCIS will accept an oral contract as evidenced by the summation of the elements of the oral agreement. Such evidence may include, but is not limited to: emails between the contractual parties, a written summation of the terms of the agreement, or any other evidence that demonstrates that an oral agreement was created. The summary of the terms of the oral agreement must contain what was offered by the employer, and what was accepted by the employee. The summary does not have to be signed by both parties to establish the oral agreement; however it must document the terms of the employment offered and the beneficiary's agreement to the offer.

The itinerary and/or petitioner letter must establish that there are events or activities in the beneficiary's field of extraordinary ability for the validity period requested. A letter from the petitioner explaining the activities is recommended and in a situation with multiple employers and/or work sites, an itinerary listing the date, location, and nature of each event is necessary.

Evidence that the beneficiary meets the regulatory criteria to qualify for an O-1A or O-1B visa needs to be submitted. If the beneficiary has received or has been nominated for a significant national or international award or prize, evidence of that should be provided. If the beneficiary has not received a significant national or international award in his or her field, the beneficiary should provide supporting evidence that he or she meets at least three of the other supporting criteria.

There are two levels of analysis USCIS applies to an O-1 petition: the beneficiary must meet the regulatory criteria and the overall definition of extraordinary ability. Simply submitting enough evidence to cover three of the criteria does not ensure a successful petition. The evidence must also show the beneficiary to be "one of a small percentage who has risen to the very top of the field of endeavor" (O-1A) or to have "a high level of achievement in the specific artistic field evidenced by a degree of skill and recognition substantially above that ordinarily encountered" (O-1B).

### Advice of Counsel

USCIS has confirmed that the correct burden of proof required of petitioners seeking immigration benefits is "preponderance of the evidence" and not the criminal law standard of "beyond a reasonable doubt." Often this comes into play with the O-1 and P-1 visa categories due to the subjective nature of the criteria. Filings are not required to demonstrate eligibility beyond a reasonable doubt.

## The O-2 Filing Requirements

If the O-1 visa beneficiary has essential support personnel that require O-2 visas, a separate I-129 form should be filed for the O-2 applicant(s). Multiple beneficiaries can be included on one I-129 form for O-2 status. While the O-2 applicants do not have to provide evidence of meeting the regulatory criteria for extraordinary ability, the petition should include a letter signed by the petitioner and evidence of the applicants' credentials and need for their services in the United States. O-2 beneficiaries are also subject to the consultation requirements.

Once the petition has been approved by USCIS, an approval notice is issued and the beneficiary is then able to appear at a U.S. consulate for the issuance of the visa. O-1 and O-2 petitions can be granted initially for up to three years, and subsequent extensions can be issued in one-year increments.

# The P Visa

This visa category is reserved for athletes and group entertainers who are entering the United States temporarily for the sole purpose of performing in a competition, event, or performance.

The P-1A visa is for athletes performing individually or as part of a group or team at an internationally recognized level of performance.

The P-1B visa is for a person who performs with or is an integral or essential part of an entertainment group that has been recognized internationally as being outstanding in the specific field for a sustained and substantial period of time. At least 75 percent of the members of the group must have had a substantial and sustained relationship with the group for at least one year. The reputation of the group, not the individual achievements of its members or the acclaim of a particular production, is essential to the P-1B.

### Example Please

U2's Bono has made individual achievements in music, but if U2 band members require P visas to perform in the United States on their next world tour, the accomplishments of the band (twenty-two Grammys and 145 million albums sold worldwide!) will be the focus of the petition.

The P-2 visa is for an artist or entertainer (individual, part of a group, or an integral part of the performance of a group) who seeks to perform under a reciprocal exchange program between an organization or organizations in the United States and an organization or organizations in one or more foreign states, and provide for the temporary exchange of artists and entertainers, or groups of artists and entertainers.

The P-3 visa is for an artist or entertainer who is coming to the United States (either individually, as part of a group, or as an integral part of the performance of a group) to perform, teach, or coach under a commercial or noncommercial program that is culturally unique.

P-4 visas are for the accompanying spouses and children of P-1, P-2, or P-3 visa holders.

The P visa category also provides status for essential support personnel who will accompany P-1, P-2, or P-3 visa holders to serve as an integral part of the performance. Specifically, the individual must perform support services that cannot be readily performed by a U.S. worker, and the services provided must be essential to the successful performance of the P-1, P-2, or P-3 visa holder.

## Internationally Recognized—and Some Exceptions

Being internationally recognized means having a high level of achievement in a field evidenced by a degree of skill and recognition substantially above that ordinarily encountered, to the extent that such achievement is renowned, leading, or well known in more than one country.

In some cases for the P-1B visa applicant, the requirements of having international recognition and a one–year relationship with the group or team may be waived. Certain nationally known entertainment groups may have the internationally recognized requirement waived if they can establish they have been recognized nationally as outstanding for a sustained amount of time in consideration of special circumstances.

The one-year-prior relationship requirement also may be waived for any performer or entertainer who replaces an essential member of the group because of urgent circumstances such as illness or because the replacement performer augments the group by performing a critical role.

## The P-1 Petition Process

To apply for a P visa, the petitioner files form I-129 with the appropriate USCIS service center—as with any other employment NIV. (As mentioned above, the O and P visas allow for agents to serve as petitioners.) Multiple beneficiaries may be included on the I-129 form if they are members of the group seeking classification or if they are essential support personnel.

All P petitions require a consultation/advisory opinion with an appropriate union. The union may submit a specific opinion or a letter of no objection. All P petitions must also include a copy of the contract or a summary of the oral contract between the petitioner and the beneficiary/group.

P-1A athlete petitioners must provide documentation showing that they will perform at an athletic competition of distinguished reputation, and that the competition requires participation of an athlete or team with international reputation. It must also be proven that the athlete or team is internationally recognized. In addition to the consultation and a copy of the contract, the petition should include evidence of at least two of the following:

> ➤ Significant participation in a prior season with a major U.S. team

> ➤ Participation in an international competition with a national team

> ➤ Participation in an athletic event in a prior season with a U.S. university or college

> ➤ A written statement from a sports media representative or an expert in the sport who confirms how the petitioner or team is internationally recognized

> ➤ A written statement from a U.S. sports team confirming that the petitioner or team is internationally recognized

> ➤ How the petitioner or team would be ranked if the sport was internationally ranked

> ➤ The petitioner or team has received a significant award or honor in the sport

P-1B performers in an entertainment group must provide documentation showing that 75 percent of the group members have had a sustained and substantial relationship with the group for at least one year. In addition to the consultation and a copy of the contract, the petition should also include an itinerary with the dates and locations of the performances, a copy of the contract between the petitioner and the beneficiary or a summary of terms of the oral agreement under which the beneficiary will be employed, documentation that the group is internationally recognized as outstanding for a sustained and substantial period of time as demonstrated by evidence of the group's receipt of or nomination for significant international awards or prizes for outstanding achievement in the field, or evidence of at least three of the following:

> ➤ That the group has performed and will perform as a starring or leading entertainment group in productions or events that have a distinguished reputation as evidenced by critical reviews, advertisements, publicity releases, publications, contracts, or endorsements

> ➤ That the group has achieved international recognition and acclaim for outstanding achievement in its field as evidenced by reviews in major newspapers, trade journals, magazines, or other published material

➤ That the group has performed and will perform services as a leading or starring group for organizations and establishments that have a distinguished reputation as evidenced by articles in newspapers, trade journals, publications, or testimonials

➤ That the group has a record of major commercial or critically acclaimed successes as evidenced by indicators such as ratings; box office receipts; record, cassette, or video sales; and other achievements as reported in trade journals, major newspapers, or other publications

➤ That the group has received significant recognition for achievements from critics, organizations, government agencies, or other recognized experts in the field.

➤ That the group has commanded and will command a high salary or other substantial remuneration for services comparable to others similarly situated in the field as evidenced by contracts or other reliable evidence.

## P-2 Visas

The P-2 visa petition must provide documentation that the artist/entertainer is entering the United States temporarily to perform individually, as part of a group, or as an integral part of a performance under a government-recognized reciprocal exchange program. In addition to the consultation, the filing should include the following documents:

➤ A copy of the formal reciprocal exchange agreement between the sponsoring U.S. organization(s) and the organization(s) in the foreign country that will receive the U.S. artist or entertainer

➤ An itinerary listing the date, location, and details of each event/performance if they will be taking place in multiple areas

➤ A written statement from the sponsoring organization describing the reciprocal exchange of U.S. artists or entertainers

➤ Evidence that the beneficiary and the U.S. artist/entertainer who are engaged in the reciprocal exchange agreement are artists of comparable skills and that the terms and conditions of employment are similar

➤ A U.S. labor organization was involved in negotiating or has concurred with the reciprocal exchange of U.S. and foreign artists or entertainers

## P-3 Visas

The P-3 visa petition must show that the individual or group is entering the United States temporarily to develop, interpret, represent, coach, or teach a unique or traditional ethnic, folk, cultural, musical, theatrical, or artistic performance or presentation. It must also show that the cultural event will further the understanding or development of the individual's or group's art form. The program may be of a commercial or noncommercial nature, and a P-3 group does not have to provide evidence that it existed prior to the tour/event in the United States. The filing should include the following documents:

> ➤ An explanation of the event and an itinerary listing the date, location, and details of each event/performance if the events will be taking place in multiple areas

> ➤ Affidavits, testimonials, or letters from recognized experts attesting to the authenticity of the individual/group's skills in performing, presenting, coaching, or teaching the unique and traditional art forms

> ➤ Documentation that the U.S. events/performances or presentations will be culturally unique events

> ➤ Documentation that the individual/group's performance is culturally unique as evidenced by reviews in newspapers, journals, or other published materials

Essential support personnel of P visa holders are required to file a separate form I-129, and the petition must include a consultation from an appropriate labor organization. The petitioner should also submit a statement describing the support person's prior and current critical skills and experience with the primary P visa beneficiary. A copy of a written contract between the employer and the support person or a summary of the terms of the oral agreement under which the support person will be employed should also be provided.

Once the petition has been approved by USCIS, an approval notice is issued, and the beneficiary/group is then able to appear at a U.S. consulate for the issuance of a visa.

P-1 athletes may be admitted for a period of up to five years with one extension up to five years. P-1 petitions for athletic teams and entertainment groups may not exceed one year. P-2, P-3, and essential support personnel are granted admission for the time necessary to complete the event outlined on the I-129 up to one year. Spouses and children in P-4 status may be admitted for the same period of time as the beneficiary/group but may not engage in employment.

# CHAPTER 12

# The NAFTA Visa for Canadian and Mexican Professionals

## In This Chapter

➤ The TN visa

➤ Canadian citizens' TN visa requirements

➤ Mexican citizens' TN visa requirements

The North American Free Trade Agreement (NAFTA) was signed in 1992 to create special economic and trade relationships between the United States, Canada, and Mexico. As part of NAFTA, the TN (trade NAFTA) nonimmigrant classification was created to allow qualified Canadian and Mexican citizens to seek temporary entry into the United States to engage in business activities at a profession*al level. Another way of thinking about the TN visa is that it is an H-1B for Canadians and Mexicans.

The TN visa is unique in that Canadian citizens who qualify generally are not required to obtain a visa stamp to enter the United States and work in TN status. Put differently, although Canadians may be admitted to the United States and hold TN visa status, they won't actually have any visa at all.

**Visa Vocab**

NAFTA defines "business activities at a professional level" as undertakings requiring the individual to have at least a bachelor's degree or other appropriate credentials demonstrating status as a professional.

# TN Visa Eligibility

In general, Canadian and Mexican citizens are eligible for TN status if:

> ➤ their profession qualifies under the regulations;

> ➤ the U.S. position requires a NAFTA professional;

> ➤ the beneficiary has the qualifications for the profession; and

> ➤ there is a prearranged full-time or part-time job with a U.S. employer.

Being self-employed is not permitted for the TN visa. But if a self-employed beneficiary has partial or controlling interest in a Canadian company that has contracted with a U.S. company to perform management consulting services, the beneficiary may be granted TN status.

### Advice of Counsel

The doctrine of dual intent is not applicable to TN visa beneficiaries and their dependent family members. Should a TN visa applicant eventually decide to pursue permanent residency, a change of status to another work visa category, such as an H-1B visa, would need to be considered.

# The NAFTA List of Professions (aka Appendix 1603.D.1)

As noted above, the TN visa is similar to the H-1B visa in that it is reserved for professionals. However, unlike the H-1B visa the TN visa has very specific rules as to exactly what type of jobs it considers professional in nature.

In fact, a specific list of professional jobs and their educational requirements was created under the NAFTA Treaty. If your job falls into one of the listed categories, you may be eligible for a TN visa. If not, you probably aren't. The first step in finding out whether you may qualify for a TN visa is to see if your job is on the list, which can be found in Appendix E.

### Advice of Counsel

Many IT professionals may call themselves (or are called by their employer) software engineers. However, beneficiaries applying under this classification are strongly recommended to have a degree, such as a computer engineering degree, specifically indicating a course of study in engineering. If the beneficiary has a bachelor's degree in computer science or computer information systems, he or she may want to consider applying under the computer systems analyst classification.

### Management Consultants

While the NAFTA appendix is a bit vague on the management consultant classification, USCIS has narrowed the definition of who qualifies for and what constitutes a management consultant position. The USCIS *NAFTA Handbook* (which provides guidance to port of entry officers on how to adjudicate TN applications) specifies that: "Management consultants provide services directed towards improving the managerial, operating, and economic performance of public and private entities by analyzing and resolving strategic and operating problems and thereby improving the entity's goals, objectives, policies, strategies, administration, organization, and operation." If the beneficiary will be a salaried employee of the U.S. company, the U.S. position should be a supernumerary, temporary position.

# The TN Process for Canadian Citizens

Canadian citizens seeking initial entry to the United States are not required to file a petition with USCIS for TN status. Applications are made directly at the applicable port of entry, such as a border crossing or an airport via preflight inspection or a land-crossing point.

Also, Canadian citizens are visa exempt—they don't actually need a visa at all. As you can imagine, this makes the TN visa extremely efficient for qualifying Canadian professionals.

When submitting paperwork for a TN visa, the beneficiary should carry proof of Canadian citizenship (valid Canadian passport) as well as a letter from the TN petitioner in the United States. This letter should detail the terms of the prospective employment such as describing

**Visa Vocab**

Being visa exempt means you are not required to obtain a visa.

the professional job, the purpose of the employment, the intended length of stay, and the beneficiary's educational qualifications. The beneficiary should also provide evidence of his or her educational or alternative credentials for the specific NAFTA job classification (copy of degree, transcript, state/provisional license, work experience letters). If the beneficiary's degree was issued from a college or university outside of Canada or the United States, it is advisable to provide documentation from a professional evaluation service confirming that the degree is equivalent to a degree conferred by an accredited U.S. college or university.

Since Canadians aren't given a visa, what are they given to show they have TN status? Once approved, the beneficiary is issued a white I-94 card, as with any other NIV, but the I-94 card is stamped for multiple entries. The beneficiary should retain this I-94 card and not surrender it each time he or she leaves the United States. Also, the officer should annotate the back of the I-94 card with the beneficiary's NAFTA job classification as well as the TN employer in the United States. The TN is employer specific; any change in employer renders the TN status void, again, as is the case with most employment-based NIVs.

### Canadian Dependents

Spouses and unmarried children under the age of twenty-one of TN visa applicants are eligible to apply for TD status to enter the United States. TD applicants should also have proof of Canadian citizenship when applying at the border and should carry evidence of their relationship to the TN beneficiary such as a marriage or birth certificate issued by a civil or government authority (religious certificates are generally not accepted). If a spouse or dependent child is not a Canadian citizen, he or she is still eligible for TD status but must apply for a TD visa at a U.S. consulate and cannot apply at the port of entry. Spouses and children cannot work while in the United States, but they are permitted to study.

Canadian TN and TD applicants are eligible for initial status for up to three years. Extensions of status may be processed with USCIS using form I-129 or at a U.S. port of entry, and while the extensions may only be requested and granted in up to three-year increments, there is no limitation on how many times the TN may be extended. If a Canadian citizen is currently in the United States and seeking a change of status from another work classification to TN, an I-129 petition may be filed on his or her behalf, or the beneficiary may leave the United States and process at a U.S. port of entry. If the I-129 petition is filed for a change of status, the beneficiary cannot begin employment with the new company until the I-129 is approved and the I-797 approval notice is issued.

# The TN Process for Mexican Citizens

Mexican citizens are also not required to file a petition with USCIS for TN status, but they are required to appear at a U.S. consulate to apply for a visa. Put differently, Mexican citizens are not visa exempt, which makes the TN category not that much different or more efficient than the H-1B visa category for many Mexican professionals. The visa application process requires both the standard visa application documents (DS-160, photo, fees, etc.) as well as the following supporting documentation:

➤ Evidence of the applicant's educational or alternative credentials applicable for the NAFTA job classification, such as a copy of a degree, a transcript, a state or provisional license, or work experience letters

➤ Letter or contract from the U.S. petitioning employer stating that the position in the United States requires the employment of a person in a professional capacity consistent with NAFTA's Appendix 1603.d.1; and the exact duties and educational requirements of the U.S. position, the beneficiary's educational qualifications or appropriate credentials for the position, the intended salary, and the anticipated length of stay.

## Mexican Dependents

Spouses and unmarried children under the age of twenty-one of TN visa applicants are eligible to apply for entry in TD dependent status, and they must appear for an interview with the U.S. consulate. A spouse or dependent child who is not a Mexican citizen is still eligible for TD status. TD applicants should provide evidence if their relationship to the TN beneficiary such as a marriage or birth certificate issued by a civil or government authority (religious certificates are generally not accepted). Spouses and children cannot work while in the United States, but they are permitted to study.

## TN Validity

Currently, because of reciprocity agreements between the United States and Mexico, TN and TD applicants are issued a visa valid for one year, although these are subject to indefinite renewals.

### Advice of Counsel

Reciprocity agreements govern how long a visa for Canadian or Mexicans can be issued. The Canadian and Mexican governments issue visas of the same length to U.S. citizens—hence, reciprocity. These reciprocity tables are updated periodically, and the most recent information on reciprocity agreements can be found at the DOS's website.

Once the TN beneficiary is in the United States, extensions of status may be processed with USCIS using form I-129. As with Canadian TNs, extensions may be requested and granted in up to three-year increments, and there is no limitation on how many times the TN may be extended. In other words, an individual can in theory keep a TN visa forever, which makes it quite beneficial.

Keep in mind that while the TN status may be extended for three years while the beneficiary remains in the United States, the visa stamp in the passport must be renewed to allow for travel.

If a Mexican citizen is currently in the United States and is seeking a change of status from another work classification to TN status, an I-129 petition may be filed by the sponsoring employer, or the Mexican citizen may leave the United States and process the change of status at a U.S. consulate. If the I-129 petition is filed for a change of status, the beneficiary cannot begin employment with the new company until the I-129 is approved and the I-797 approval notice is issued.

# PART FOUR

## Visas for Tourists, Nannies, Students, and Trainees

# CHAPTER 13

# The F-1 and M-1 Visas for Students

---

### In This Chapter

➤ Visas for academic studies

➤ Meeting the school's admissions criteria

➤ Entering the United States

➤ Keeping your student status

➤ Employment options for students

➤ What happens after graduation

---

Foreign students come to the United States, often for the first time in their lives, to obtain the best education possible. In the process of navigating their courses and the culture shock, they are expected to maintain a visa status that is an anomaly in comparison to most other visa categories.

## The Student Visa

F-1 and M-1 visas are for students pursuing a "full course of study" toward a specific educational or professional objective. The most common use of F-1 visas is for students attending U.S. colleges or universities. However, F-1–designated programs also include language training programs, conservatories, seminaries, and private elementary and high schools. The M-1 visa is specifically for students in vocational or other nonacademic programs other than language training.

Students with F-1 and M-1 visas can only attend academic or vocational schools that have been designated by the Department of Homeland Security (DHS) as schools open to F-1 and/or M-1 students. These schools are authorized to issue the appropriate documentation to the student.

Now you might wonder why the schools issue the visa status documentation. Didn't those other visa categories discussed in earlier chapters require a petition approved by USCIS?

Correct, and that is just one of the many exceptions that comes with the F-1 and M-1 visa categories.

### Visa Vocab

The principal designated school official (PDSO) is the person who handles or supervises visa matters for a school.

### Visa Vocab

SEVIS is an Internet database administered by DHS and updated by PSDOs and DSOs that tracks information about students. Officers at ports of entry, U.S. consulates, and service centers are also required to check and update SEVIS to ensure an accurate accounting of a student's status events such as entry/exit data, program extensions, and employment authorization.

# Getting Accepted

To start the process, prospective students must meet their chosen school's admissions criteria. The school reviews the student's eligibility, including academic admissibility and English language skills (a standardized English proficiency test is usually required).

Qualified students must prove to the school that they have the financial resources to meet expenses, such as tuition, fees, and living costs, while studying in the United States. Each student must show that funds exist at least for the first year of study, and that barring unforeseen circumstances adequate funding will be available for the subsequent years of study.

Once the school admits the student and eligibility is verified, the required documentation can be issued. DHS requires that each school assign a principal designated school official (PDSO) to serve as the primary DHS contact and up to nine other DSOs.

The PDSO and DSOs are responsible for reporting their F-1 and M-1 students and maintaining their records within the Student and Exchange Visitor Information System (SEVIS).

### The I-20 Form

Through SEVIS, the PDSO or a DSO issues the I-20 certificate for eligibility for nonimmigrant F-1 and M-1student status. The I-20 form serves as the student's primary status document and includes basic biographical information as well as details about the academic program, including intended major, the number of credit hours required for the full-time program, dates of study, and the details of the student's financial support.

**Advice of Counsel**

The I-20 form is as important to the student's visa status as the I-94 card is for most other NIV categories.

# Entering the United States and the Elusive D/S

With the I-20 form in hand, the student must now apply for a visa at the U.S. consulate in his or her home country. However, obtaining a student visa can be a little trickier than it is with other visa categories. Because the I-20 form is issued by schools and the student's qualifications have not been reviewed by an immigration official as with petition-based categories, students can be heavily scrutinized.

Most consular officials require a student to provide substantial supporting documentation at the interview. For example, if the student's I-20 form indicates that $20,000 is required to be available in the student's bank account to cover tuition, the officer may want to see those bank statements.

Students are also required to provide evidence of strong ties to their home country, as F-1 and M-1 are visa categories that require nonimmigrant intent. Students must show that they intend to leave the United States upon completion of their course of study and have a foreign residence that they do not intend to abandon.

The F visa is typically issued for the length of study annotated on the I-20 form, such as four years for a standard bachelor's degree program. Upon entry, the student presents his or her passport with the visa and the I-20 form. The CBP officer updates SEVIS with the entry and issues an I-94 card showing the date of entry and the expiration date of D/S.

**Visa Vocab**

*D/S* stands for "duration of status." The F-1 status is valid for as long as the student continues to meet the requirements of the program of study and until the noted expiration date.

# Maintaining Student Status

Once a student enters the United States, there are many requirements that are essential to maintaining student status. If any of these requirements are not met, the student can be deemed to have violated his or her status. Due to SEVIS requirements, important milestones in a student's program must be reported, and in many cases a new I-20 form must be generated.

## *Transfers and Withdrawals*

An F-1 student can transfer schools if he or she has been pursuing the full course of study specified on the current I-20 form and the student intends to pursue a full course of study at the new school. But a new I-20 form must be executed by a DSO at the new school, so the student must go through the admissions process for the new school and provide evidence of financial ability to attend the new school.

M-1 students can transfer schools only within the first six months unless reason for not being able to remain at the present school is due to circumstances beyond the student's control.

An F-1 student who wishes to withdraw from school is provided a fifteen-day grace period to leave the United States. If the F-1 student fails to obtain permission to withdraw, no grace period is afforded.

## *Reducing Course Load*

Students are required to maintain a full course load (typically considered twelve credit hours per semester or quarter). If the student requires a reduction in course load below the determined full course load, the student must first go to a DSO and obtain permission. Students may reduce their course load only one time unless it is for medical reasons, and then only for a maximum of twelve months for F-1 students and five months for M-1 students.

### **Example Please**

Keiko from Japan has come to the United States to study business. She begins her course of study (fourteen credit hours) but she becomes overwhelmed with her classes. So she does what some of her fellow classmates do: she goes to the registrar's office and drops a class. Unfortunately, the class Keiko dropped was three credit hours and she is now taking only eleven credit hours, which is less than the twelve credit hours listed on her I-20 form as required for a "full-time course of study." She also did not go to her DSO and obtain prior approval to reduce her course load. Because of this, she is technically no longer maintaining her F-1 status, even though her I-94 card says D/S and her I-20 form and visa are still valid for four years.

### Correcting a Status Violation

So what can a student do to correct a status violation? An application for reinstatement of status can be made to USCIS if the student meets the following criteria:

> ➤ The student has not been out of status for more than five months at the time the reinstatement request is filed

> ➤ The student does not have a record of repeated or willful status violations

> ➤ The student is currently pursuing or intends to pursue the full course of study as shown on the I-20 form

> ➤ The student has not been employed without authorization

> ➤ The student is not removable based upon any other grounds

> ➤ The student can establish that the violation resulted from circumstances beyond the student's control or the violation was related to a reduction in course load that would have been within the DSO's power to authorize, and the student would suffer extreme hardship if not reinstated.

If the student is reinstated, he or she receives a new I-20 form and may remain in the United States to continue the course of study. If the reinstatement is denied, the student will most likely have to leave the United States.

# Employment Options

Employment options for students are limited because the primary reason they are in the United States is to study. Also, when students apply for an F-1 or M-1 visa, they indicate that certain financial resources are available for the intended study.

F-1 students are not eligible for work authorization during their first year of study except for on-campus employment. While work on the school premises is permitted, it is limited to part-time while school is in session. Full-time employment is allowed during school breaks.

After the first year of study, F-1 students can engage in certain types of employment with DSO approval and SEVIS annotation.

### Severe Economic Hardship

Work authorization can be obtained if the student has severe economic hardship caused by unforeseen circumstances beyond his or her control. The student must be in good academic standing and be carrying a full course load, and an application must be made to USCIS for an employment authorization document (EAD). If approved, employment is limited to part-time while school is in session, but full-time employment is allowed during school breaks.

## *Practical Training*

F-1 students are eligible to complete training that is related to their field of study. There are two types of practical training:

> ➤ Curricular practical training (CPT): CPT is employment such as an internship, cooperative education, or practicum that is allowed only while the student is engaged in his or her academic program. CPT is allowed on a part- or full-time basis, and there is no limit to how many hours a student puts into CPT. However, if a student performs two years of part-time CPT or one year of full-time CPT, he or she is not eligible for optional practical training.

> ➤ Optional practical training (OPT): OPT can be completed while the student is in school or after graduation. It is limited to twelve months, and the student must apply with USCIS for and receive an EAD before he or she can begin this employment.

M-1 students are not allowed any employment except for OPT, which may only be obtained after completion of study. As with F-1 students, M-1 students must apply with USCIS for an EAD before employment begins. The job must be in the student's field of study, and the M-1 student can be given only one period of OPT equal to one month of each four months the student pursued the full course of study. For example, if the student's M-1 program was twelve months, he or she is eligible for three months of OPT.

# After Graduation

After completing the designated program, the student has a grace period (sixty days for F-1s and thirty days for M-1s) to leave the United States. If a student plans to work under OPT after graduation, the OPT must be requested before this grace period ends. While the student is working under OPT, he or she is still considered to be in student status.

### Advice of Counsel

Travel while working during OPT is permissible provided that the student has a valid visa stamp in his or her passport. Upon re-entry to the United States, the student must present an unexpired EAD and the properly endorsed I-20 form with the valid visa stamp. It is also advisable to carry a job offer letter or letter of employment from the employer where the OPT is being performed.

Additionally, F-1 students who completed a degree in the science, technology, engineering, or math (STEM) fields are eligible to apply for a seventeen-month extension of their OPT. This extension can only be granted if the student has a job or job offer from a U.S. employer enrolled in DHS's E-Verify program. E-Verify is an Internet-based system that allows businesses to verify the eligibility of their employees to work in the United States.

## *From Student to Professional*

Students who successfully complete their academic program and secure a job offer have the option to change their status. Many F-1 students apply for a change of status to H-1B professional worker status after completing a degree program in the United States. This is so common, in fact, that USCIS sets aside twenty thousand H-1Bs in each year's H-1B cap for individuals with advanced degrees earned from a U.S. academic institution.

M-1 students cannot change to H-1B status if their background and qualification for the H-1B was training and/or education they received as an M-1 student.

F-1 students applying for new H-1B visas will be subject to the H-1B cap unless the sponsoring employer is an institution of higher learning, affiliated research organization, nonprofit research organization, or governmental research organization. As discussed in chapter 8, the H-1B petition must be filed and receipted by USCIS before the annual quota is hit. The earliest permitted filing date is April 1 for an October 1 start date.

As most F-1 students complete their academic programs in May or June, there can be several logistical issues to consider when applying for the H-1B visa. First, at the time of filing it requires that the sponsored employee has obtained the required education, at least a bachelor's degree. For most students, May or June is the completion date of their degree program and therefore filing as early as April 1 is not possible because the required degree has not yet been obtained.

Once the H-1B is filed, the October 1 start date can also pose a problem for both the student and the H-1B employer. This timing issue is referred to as the cap gap, the gap in time between the end of school or the OPT expiration and October 1. Provided

### Example Please

Our F-1 student, Keiko, has completed her bachelor's degree in business and is now working for XYZ Corporation under OPT. Keiko's OPT will expire on June 1; however, XYZ Corp. filed an H-1B change of status petition on Keiko's behalf and it was receipted on April 1. Keiko is now eligible to remain in the United States and keep working during her cap gap time from June 1 to October 1—the start date of the H-1B.

that the H-1B petition has been filed and accepted for the annual cap before the F-1 student's grace period or OPT expires, the student is eligible to remain in the United States until the October 1 start date. There is also an automatic extension of OPT given to F-1 students who filed for a change of status to H-1B in a timely manner if that H-1B petition was accepted and receipted for the H-1B cap.

# CHAPTER 14

# The J-1 and H-3 Visas for Exchange Visitors and Trainees

## In This Chapter

➤ The trainee and the exchange visitor

➤ The H-3 trainee

➤ The J-1 exchange visitor

➤ The foreign residency requirement

Visas for those who come to the United States for training can be a bit of a catchall category. Unlike the very specific designations of the work visa category, training visas can include companies training their workers in proprietary skills, foreign physicians and researchers training at top research institutions, and teachers on scholarly exchanges. There are two visa categories that cover the majority of these types of workers: The H-3 trainee and the J-1 exchange visitor.

### Visa Vocab

The H-3 trainee visa allows the beneficiary to go to the United States to receive instruction and training in a program that isn't primarily designated to provide productive employment. The J-1 exchange visitor visa allows the beneficiary to go to the United States to train, study, teach, or participate in an educational exchange.

# H-3 Trainee Visa

The H-3 trainee visa is beneficial for U.S. employers who already have or are seeking to establish an internal training program for temporary workers at their organization. The employer has the flexibility to develop the program and does not have to meet the standards of someone else's program (as explained below with the J-1 visa).

## Training Program Requirements

There are specific criteria that the employer's training program must meet to qualify a beneficiary as an H-3 trainee. One such criterion is that the proposed training cannot be available in the H-3 trainee's home country. The training plan should specify the type of training and why it is available only in the United States. Another criterion is that the H-3 trainee cannot be placed in a position that is in the normal operation of the business in which a U.S. citizen or permanent resident worker would regularly be employed. H-3 trainees are not allowed to engage in productive employment unless it is incidental and necessary to the training. Finally, the training must clearly benefit the H-3 trainee in pursuing a career outside of the United States.

USCIS requires an established training plan with a specific objective and a schedule for the training. The amount of time spent on productive employment should be minimal. On-the-job supervised training can be included; however, it must be clearly proven that this training is educational, not productive, employment. It should also specify what training is supervised and what is unsupervised. Unsupervised training should be kept to a minimum. The training program should also state why the training program benefits the petitioning company.

Because the training must benefit the trainee's career pursuits outside of the United States, the training should provide new skills and expertise for the trainee. The training program should not be designed to recruit and train individuals to eventually staff the company's U.S. operations. To that effect, H-3 trainees are admitted only for the length of the training program, which can be no longer than two years.

## How to Apply for the H-3 Trainee Visa

The U.S. employer files an I-129 petition with the appropriate USCIS service center in the United States. The training plan should be included with the petition along with evidence of the trainee's background. If the company has more than one trainee for whom it is seeking H-3 status, multiple beneficiaries can be included on the petition.

Once the petition is approved, the H-3 trainee(s) must appear at a U.S. consulate to have a visa issued. H-3 trainees who are in the United States for the maximum two years are not eligible for an extension, change of status, or readmission to the United States in H or L status unless they have resided and been physically present outside of the United States for at least six months.

# J-1 Exchange Visitor Visa

J-1 exchange visitors are sponsored by an entity designated by the DOS to act as a J-1 exchange program. Foreign nationals apply to the J-1 program, and if the applicant meets the program's criteria as well as the regulatory guidelines, the applicant is approved to participate in the specific program. The J-1 program then issues a DS-2019 certificate of eligibility for exchange visitor status through USCIS's Student and Exchange Visitor Information System (SEVIS). The applicant then takes the DS-2019 certificate to the U.S. consulate in his or her home country to have the J-1 visa issued.

J-1 participants must demonstrate that they have nonimmigrant intent and English language skills that will allow them to function on a day-to-day basis in the designated J-1 program. They must provide evidence of sufficient funds and medical insurance to cover their stay in the United States.

**Visa Vocab**

The DS-2019 form is the sponsor-issued document that allows J-1 exchange visitors to appear at a U.S. consulate to apply for a visa.

The visa is issued for the length of study annotated on the DS-2019 form; however, once the beneficiary enters the United States, an I-94 card is issued for duration of status (D/S). Duration of status for J-1 exchange visitors is the length of stay required to complete their program, which is shown on their DS-2019 form, plus thirty days of grace period at the end of their stay. J-1 visitors have a responsibility to meet the program's requirements to ensure they properly maintain status while in the United States.

# Common J-1 Subcategories

The J-1 exchange visitor classification covers a wide range of subcategories, and each subcategory has different requirements and criteria. Here we focus on a few of the most common subcategories.

## *Au Pairs*

This subcategory allows foreign nationals eighteen through twenty-six years old to be placed with U.S. citizen host families. Au pairs provide limited childcare services for the family while also completing academic credit or its equivalent at an accredited U.S. postsecondary educational institution. They cannot work more than ten hours per day, and not more than a total of forty-five hours per week.

There are limitations on the types of childcare au pairs may provide. For example, au pairs cannot be placed with a family that has an infant younger than three months old unless a parent or other responsible adult is at home during the intended childcare hours.

### Advice of Counsel

An au pair may work with a special-needs child only if the au pair has proven prior experience, skill, or training in caring for special-needs children.

Host families must pay the au pair in accordance with DOL guidelines for this type of work and are required to contribute toward the cost of the au pair's required academic course work. An agreement between the host family and the au pair must be signed prior to the au pair's placement in the United States.

Au pairs are eligible for up to twelve months on their J-1 program and may be granted a one-time extension of status for six, nine, or twelve months. An au pair may seek to return to the program for a new twelve-month period after remaining outside of the United States for a two years.

## *Trainees and Interns*

J-1 trainees and interns are professionals and students seeking training directly related to their occupational field. They are placed with U.S. employers to perform training in one of the following fields:

> ➤ Agriculture, forestry, and fishing

> ➤ Arts and culture

> ➤ Construction and building trades

> ➤ Education, social science, library science, counseling, and social services

> ➤ Health-related occupations

> ➤ Hospitality and tourism

> ➤ Information media and communications

➤ Management, business, commerce, and finance

➤ Public administration and law

➤ Science, engineering, architecture, mathematics, and industrial occupations

J-1 trainees must have a degree or professional certificate from a foreign postsecondary academic institution and at least one year of related work experience abroad, or at least five years of experience abroad in an occupational field. Trainees are eligible to stay in the United States for up to eighteen months on their J-1 program, except for those in the agriculture and hotel and tourism fields, who are limited to twelve months.

J-1 interns must currently be pursuing a degree at a postsecondary academic institution abroad or have graduated from such an institution no more than twelve months before the start date of the intended J-1 program. Interns are eligible for up to twelve months of stay.

## Teachers

Foreign teachers seeking to come to the United States to teach full-time at an accredited primary or secondary school may qualify for a J-1 visa if they have a minimum of three years of teaching experience or related professional experience. J-1 teachers must meet the qualifications for teaching in primary or secondary school in their home country and show they are of good character and reputation. They must also satisfy the standards to teach in the U.S. state where they will be teaching under the J-1 exchange program. J-1 teachers are eligible for up to three years of stay.

## Foreign Physicians

Those seeking clinical training as a J-1 physician receive graduate medical education or training at accredited schools of medicine or other scientific institutions. Generally, this type of training falls under one of two types: clinical training and nonclinical training.

J-1 physicians seeking clinical training must have adequate prior education and training, pass qualifying exams, and show competency in oral and written English. Applicants are also required to provide a statement of need from the government of the country of their nationality or last legal permanent residence. An agreement or contract from a U.S. accredited medical school, an affiliated hospital, or a scientific institution that is intended to provide the accredited medical education is also required.

**Visa Vocab**

Foreign physicians seeking clinical training in the J-1 exchange visitor category are known as foreign medical graduates (FMGs) or international medical graduates (IMGs).

The Educational Commission for Foreign Medical Graduates (ECFMG) oversees all J-1 physicians performing clinical training in the United States. ECFMG re-evaluates physicians and their eligibility for the program, requiring them to apply for renewed visa sponsorship typically on an annual basis.

J-1 physicians are eligible for up to seven years to complete their program; however, they are usually provided the "time typically required" to complete the program in accordance with the minimum number of training years required for specialty or subspecialty certification. J-1 physicians in the ECFMG program are also required to return to their home country or country of last residence for at least two years following their training. This is called the foreign residency requirement and is explained below.

Nonclinical training as a J-1 research scholar is specifically for physicians and FMGs coming to the United States to observe, consult, teach, or conduct research. The sponsoring U.S. university or academic medical center must certify that the J-1 research scholar will not be involved in any element of patient care.

## *Research Scholars and Professors*

The research scholar subcategory is not limited to physicians and FMGs. It is also available for individuals conducting research, observing, or consulting in other occupational fields. J-1 research scholars are engaged in specific projects at research institutions, corporate research facilities, accredited universities, or similar types of institutions. The professor subcategory is for an individual who is engaged primarily in teaching, lecturing, observing, or consulting at accredited postsecondary academic institutions, museums, libraries, or similar institutions.

### Advice of Counsel

A J-1 professor or research scholar cannot be a candidate for a tenure track position at the sponsoring institution.

The maximum period of stay is five years unless the research scholar or professor is directly sponsored by a federally funded national research and development center or a U.S. federal laboratory. Certain restrictions are in place for repeat participation. There is a twelve-month bar prohibiting foreign nationals from beginning a new program as a research scholar or professor if they were in the United States on a J visa for six months or more within the twelve-month period immediately preceding the start date of the new program. A twenty-four-month bar takes effect for J-1 professors and research scholars when they have completed their program and the program participation end date is recorded in SEVIS, even if the program is less than five years. These bars are different from the two-year foreign residency requirement.

# The Two-Year Foreign Residency Requirement

Certain J-1 exchange visitors are required to return to their home country or country of last residence for two years upon completion of their training program in the United States. This requirement applies to the following J visa holders:

> ➤ Participants in graduate medical education or training programs: Exchange visitors who came to the United States or acquired J status after January 10, 1997, to receive graduate medical education or training

> ➤ Participants in government-funded exchange programs: Exchange visitors in programs that were financed in whole or in part directly or indirectly by the U.S. government or the government of the exchange visitor's nationality or last residence

> ➤ Participants engaged in training covered by the skills list: Exchange visitors receiving training in a field that has been deemed a necessary skill to the development of their home country or their last country of permanent residence, as shown on the exchange visitor skills list

### Advice of Counsel

J-1 exchange visitors who are subject to the foreign residency requirement have an annotation on their visa stamp and DS-2019 form. Those J-1 visa holders who are not sure if they are subject to the foreign residency requirement can request an advisory opinion from DOS's office of visa services to confirm the applicability of the residency requirement to their J-1 program.

The two-year foreign residency requirement often comes into play when a J-1 visa holder is interested in changing status to work in the United States. The requirement must be met before a J-1 visitor is eligible for certain types of U.S. visas, such as H-1B or L-1, and before the exchange visitor may apply for legal permanent residence (aka the green card).

The J-1 visitor has the option to apply for a waiver of the two-year foreign residency requirement under one of the following categories:

➤ No objection statement: The applicant has received a no objection statement from his or her home country confirming that there is no objection to the applicant's decision not to return home.

➤ Exceptional hardship: The applicant's departure from the United States would impose exceptional hardship on a spouse or child who is a U.S. citizen or legal permanent resident.

➤ Possible persecution: The applicant would be subject to racial, religious, or political persecution upon return to his or her home country.

➤ International medical graduates: The applicant is a foreign medical graduate who is to be employed at a health care facility in a designated health care professional shortage area or at a health care facility that serves patients from such a designated area.

➤ Interested government agency: A U.S. agency has shown that granting the waiver is in the public interest and that compliance with the residency requirement would clearly be detrimental to a program or activity of official interest to the agency.

An applicant must first file with the DOS for a favorable recommendation. Once the recommendation is granted, it is sent to USCIS for a final adjudication.

# CHAPTER 15

# The K-1 and K-3 Visas for Fiancé(e)s and Spouses of U.S. Citizens

## In This Chapter

> The K-1 fiancé(e) visa

> The K-3 (spouse of a U.S. citizen) visa

> Potential issues

> The green card and maintaining residency

The K visas are all about foreign nationals becoming engaged and married to U.S. citizens. They are available to qualified U.S. citizens who want to sponsor a fiancé(e) or spouse's entry to the United States from another country.

## K-1 Visas

K-1 visas are reserved for foreign-born citizens engaged to marry U.S. citizens. The U.S. citizen is considered the sponsoring petitioner and the K-1 fiancé(e) is required to marry the sponsoring petitioner within ninety days of entering the United States on the K-1 visa. Unmarried minor children (under the age of twenty-one) of the fiancé(e) are eligible to apply for a K-2 visa to accompany the K-1 visa holder to the United States. Once the marriage is finalized in the United States, the K-1 visa holder and dependent K-2 children are eligible to apply for permanent residency via the I-485 application to register permanent residence form.

### *Who is a K-1 Fiancé(e) and Who is Not*

While fiancé(e)s of U.S. citizens are eligible for K-1 visas, this is not so for fiancé(e)s of permanent residents (green card holders) or nonimmigrant visa holders (such as H-1B or L-1). A fiancé(e) or cohabiting partner of a nonimmigrant visa holder who wishes to travel to the United States may want to consider applying for a B-2 visitor visa as a nonspousal partner (described in chapter 7).

The K-1 visa is required only if the foreign national fiancé(e) is residing outside of the United States and needs to enter the United States. If the U.S. citizen's fiancé(e) is already in the United States pursuant to another legal status, a fiancé(e) visa is not required.

To qualify for the K-1 visa, it must be shown that there is a bona fide intention to marry within ninety days of the fiancé(e)'s entry to the United States. The U.S. citizen and the K-1 visa applicant must also have no legal impediments to the marriage, and the marriage must be legally possible according to the laws of the U.S. state in which the marriage will take place. The K-1 visa applicant and the U.S. citizen also must have met in person within the past two years. USCIS may waiver the in-person requirement based on extreme hardship for the U.S. citizen sponsor to personally meet his or her fiancé(e), or if meeting would violate strict and long-established customs of the foreign culture of the fiancé(e).

# K-3 Visas

The K-3 visa is for a foreign-born citizen who has married a U.S. citizen and intends to immigrate to the United States.

When a U.S. citizen marries a foreign citizen, the U.S. citizen is immediately eligible to file an immigrant petition for his or her spouse's green card; however, if the foreign-born spouse is outside of the United States, he or she cannot enter the United States without a visa or the actual green card. The K-3 visa is meant to alleviate this issue by allowing the foreign citizen spouse to enter the United States and await the approval of the immigrant visa petition. Dependent children (unmarried children under the age of twenty-one) of K-3 visa applicants are eligible to apply for K-4 visas.

A spouse is a legally wedded husband or wife; a marriage certificate issued by a civil authority is required as proof of the marriage (religious certificates are not sufficient evidence of a marriage). Cohabitating partners and same sex marriages are currently not recognized by U.S. immigration law for the purpose of immigrating to the United States. Common-law spouses may qualify as spouses for immigration purposes depending on the laws of the country where the common-law marriage occurs.

# The K-1 and K-3 Petition Process

K-1 sponsors are required to file an I-129F form; an I-130 petition is not required. K-2 and K-4 children are not required to submit a separate I-129 petition; however, they must be listed on the petition filed with USCIS.

For the K-1 visa, both the petitioner and the fiancé(e) should submit evidence of the relationship such as correspondence between the couple and dated photos of meeting or traveling together. The K-3 visa requires the sponsor to submit a copy of the I-797 approval receipt for the I-130 petition as well as proof of the marriage. If the petitioner has a criminal record, certified copies of court and police records showing dispositions must be provided.

## Advice of Counsel

USCIS may disclose to the fiancé(e) the U.S. citizen petitioner's criminal history if it involved violence or sex offenses. If USCIS does disclose this information, the fact of the disclosure must be provided in writing to the petitioner.

As the K-3 sponsor, the U.S. citizen must first file an I-130 petition for alien relative. USCIS then issues an I-797 notice of action as a receipt for the I-130 petition.

The next step is for the K-3 sponsor to file an I-129F petition for alien fiancé(e). Don't be confused by the name of the form; this petition is used for both foreign-born fiancé(e)s and foreign citizen spouses.

If USCIS approves the I-130 petition before the I-129F, the K-3 visa will not be issued because the foreign citizen spouse no longer needs it. If USCIS notifies the National Visa Center (NVC) of an approved I-130 petition and an approved I-129F petition for the same applicant, the K-3 visa case will be administratively closed. The NVC will contact the U.S. citizen sponsor and foreign citizen spouse with instructions for processing an immigrant visa based upon the approved I-130.

Once approved, both the K-1 and K-3 petitions are valid for four months. Within that time, the fiancé(e) and sponsored spouse are expected to appear at a U.S. consulate to have the K-1 or K-3 visa issued. The petition can be revalidated in four-month increments if necessary.

The approved K-1 or K-3 petition is then sent to the DOS's NVC for processing. The K-1 is sent to the NVC that notifies the U.S. consulate in the fiancé(e)'s home country. For the K-3, the NVC is responsible for notifying the appropriate U.S. consulate of the I-129F petition approval. The foreign-born spouse is expected to appear at a U.S. consulate to have the K-3 visa issued within the valid period of the petition. The petition can be extended by the consular officer if the visa processing is not completed before the expiration.

A foreign citizen who marries a U.S. citizen outside of the United States must apply for a K-3 visa in the country where the marriage took place. If the marriage took place in the United States, the NVC sends the petition to the U.S. consulate that issues visas in the foreign-born spouse's country of nationality. If the marriage took place in a country that does not have a U.S. consulate, or if the consulate in that country does not issue visas, the NVC will send the petition to the U.S. consulate that normally processes visas for citizens of that country.

# The K Visa Process

Because the K-1 visa allows the fiancé(e) to enter the United States for the purpose of marrying a U.S. citizen and applying for permanent residency via the I-485 form, the fiancé(e) as well as any dependent children applying for K-2 visas must meet some of the requirements of an immigrant visa. For example, every K visa applicant (K-1, K-3, K-2, and K-4), regardless of age, must undergo a medical examination performed by an authorized panel physician. Each consulate has a list of appropriate physicians within the country who can perform the authorized medical exam.

The K-1 and K-3 visa applicant is also required to present evidence that he or she will not become a public charge in the United States. This can include evidence that the applicant has his or her own financial support or that the U.S. citizen petitioner is able to provide support.

Following the marriage, the U.S. citizen K-1 petitioner is required to submit an affidavit of support, the I-864 form, to USCIS with the application for permanent residency. Most consulates request the supporting documentation (visa forms, financial support documents, medical examination) to be provided first, in which case the K-1 visa applicant is contacted when the consul is ready to perform the visa interview.

Upon approval, the consulate issues a K visa stamp in the applicant's passport. K visas are issued for a single entry to the United States with a validity of six months, which means the K-1 visa holder has six months to enter the United States. Upon entry, the fiancé(e) holding the K-1 visa and any dependents are given a stay of ninety days, and the fiancé(e) and U.S. citizen have ninety days to marry. Any children entering the United States with a K-2 or K-4 visa must enter at the same time as the K-1 or K-3 parent, or after the parent's initial entry on the K-1 visa.

### Advice of Counsel

Upon entering the United States, the K-1 visa holder may immediately apply for an employment authorization document (EAD), but it is valid for only ninety days.

K-1 visa holders cannot change status to another nonimmigrant visa category, and extensions of stay cannot be requested. If the marriage does not occur within ninety days of the fiancé(e)'s entry to the United States, the K-1 visa holder and any dependent K-2 visa holders are required to leave the United States.

K-3 and K-4 visa holders are admitted to the United States for a two-year status period. This status will be terminated if one of the following occurs:

➤ The K-3 spouse divorces the U.S. citizen spouse

➤ The underlying I-130 petition is denied or revoked

➤ The K-4 child marries

➤ The green card application (the I-485 application to register permanent residence or adjust status) is denied or revoked

An extension of K-3 and K-4 status can be granted in two-year increments if the I-130 petition has not been approved or the K-3 applicant has applied for adjustment of status and that application has not been approved.

Employment authorization for K-3 and K-4 visa holders is incident to their status; however, they are required to apply for an employment authorization document.

Travel outside of the United States is possible for K-3 and K-4 visa holders as long as their current visa is valid and they intend to return to the United States using that valid K visa.

# Potential Issues

As you can imagine, problems can arise in such a complex process. It's best to be prepared.

## The K-1 Consulate Interview

One area in which problems can arise is during the consulate interview. The consular officer will ask a series of questions to determine the legitimacy of the relationship between the U.S. citizen sponsor and the K-1 visa applicant. The K-1 visa applicant should be prepared to discuss the evolution of the relationship such as how and where the couple met, plans for the wedding in the United States, plans for living arrangements and children, as well as answer questions about the U.S. citizen sponsor such as what he or she does for a living, if he or she has been married before, and if he or she has children. It is the consular officer's job to assess the relationship and determine (within a matter of minutes) if the applicant is sincere and honest and if the relationship is legitimate.

## *Vaccinations*

While not required at the time of the medical examination for the K visa, documentation of certain vaccinations is required after the marriage is completed in the United States and the adjustment of status process begins.

During the adjustment of status process, K-1 and K-3 applicants must show proof of having received the following vaccines:

➤ Mumps

➤ Measles

➤ Rubella

➤ Polio

➤ Tetanus and diphtheria toxoids

➤ Pertussis

➤ Influenza

➤ Hepatitis B

➤ Haemophilius influenza type B

➤ Varicella

➤ Pneumococcus

➤ Rotavirus

➤ Hepatitis A

➤ Meningococcus

The applicant must have had these vaccinations before the adjustment of status process can be filed.

---

### Advice of Counsel

K visa applicants should plan ahead and review the vaccination requirements during the visa process to avoid delays later.

---

## The International Marriage Broker Regulation (IMBRA)

As part the Violence Against Women and Department of Justice Reauthorization Act of 2005, a U.S. citizen petitioning for a K-1 visa for a fiancé(e) or a K-3 visa for an alien spouse must provide information on any criminal convictions for any of the following specified crimes:

➤ Domestic violence, sexual assault, child abuse and neglect, dating violence, elder abuse, and stalking

➤ Murder, manslaughter, rape, abusive sexual contact, sexual exploitation, incest, torture, trafficking, peonage, holding hostage, involuntary servitude, slave trade, kidnapping, abduction, unlawful criminal restraint, false imprisonment, or an attempt to commit any of these crimes

➤ Crimes relating to alcohol or a controlled substance for which the petitioner has been convicted on at least three occasions and where such crimes did not arise from a single act

Another function of IMBRA is to limit the number of petitions a U.S. citizen may file or have approved for a K-1 fiancé(e). If the U.S. citizen has filed two or more K-1 visa petitions at any time in the past or has previously had a K-1 visa petition approved within two years prior to the filing of the current petition, the U.S. citizen must request a waiver of those limitations. At the time the I-129F petition is filed, the

### Example Please

A U.S. citizen petitioner previously filed an I-129F for his Russian citizen fiancée; however, his fiancée was unable to enter the United States for several months due to severe illness, and the original petition expired. The petitioner requested a waiver of the filing limitations, filing a new I-129F form for the same fiancée. With the new petition, he submitted a report from a physician detailing his fiancée's illness. Since the petitioner has no criminal history, the waiver was granted.

U.S. citizen petitioner may attach a signed, dated letter requesting the waiver and explaining why a waiver would be appropriate in his or her circumstances together with any evidence in support of the waiver request. USCIS may waive the applicable time and/or numerical limitations if justification exists for such a waiver, except when the petitioner has a history of violent criminal offenses against a person or persons.

# What's Next?

Once married, it's time to apply for permanent residency via the adjustment of status process. The K-1 fiancé(e) is now a spouse of a U.S. citizen and therefore qualifies as an immediate relative. And, of course, the K-3 applicant and any K-2 and K-4 dependents are eligible to apply for permanent residency. The permanent residency application includes both the I-130 alien relative petition and the I-485 application to register permanent residence. A separate I-485 must be submitted for each applicant regardless of age.

The I-485 application can be filed provided that the applicant has maintained legal status while in United States. Each applicant must be physically present in the United States when the I-485 documentation is filed with USCIS. Each applicant may apply for EAD and travel authorization (advance parole) to permit work and travel abroad while the I-485 is pending adjudication.

### Visa Vocab

Advance parole is permission granted by the DHS to K-1 visa holders so they can return to the U.S. after travel abroad. It must be requested and approved before the visa holder leaves the United States.

Every I-485 applicant must complete a medical examination with a USCIS-approved physician to ensure the applicant is not inadmissible to the United States on public health grounds. This medical examination is in addition to the exam completed for the K visa issuance.

An I-864 affidavit of support form must also be submitted with the I-485 to show that the sponsored foreign national spouse and any dependent children have adequate financial support to live in the United States without becoming a public charge.

The I-864 form is executed by the U.S. citizen spouse, and supporting documentation such as employment letter, pay statements, and W-2 forms should be provided as evidence of income. The income of another person in the household may be used as long as that person is eligible to execute an I-864A contract between sponsor and household member. The petition is filed with USCIS and the applicant is called to appear for biometrics.

While the adjustment of status is pending, the advance parole and EAD are issued. The applicant(s) should not travel abroad until the advance parole is issued. If the applicant leaves the United States without first securing the advance parole, USCIS can consider that departure as abandonment of the permanent residency petition.

Once the petition has been adjudicated, USCIS will notify the applicant(s) to appear at their local USCIS office for a final interview. The U.S. citizen sponsor is required to appear for the interview as well, and the applicant is notified at the interview if the residency has been approved.

**Visa Vocab**

Biometrics, or fingerprinting, allows USCIS to conduct an FBI criminal background check and is done at a local USCIS application support center.

# The Green Card and Beyond

At the time of the interview, whether through IV consular processing (discussed below) or adjustment of status, if the U.S. citizen and the foreign-born spouse have been married for two years or longer, the green card issued will be valid for ten years. If the marriage has been less than two years, the applicant will be issued conditional permanent residency, and the green card will be valid for two years.

Within 120 days of the expiration date of the conditional permanent residency, the applicant must file a request to remove the conditions of the residency. At that time, USCIS will in essence reconfirm that the marriage is bona fide. Upon removal of the conditions, USCIS will issue a new permanent resident card that is valid for ten years.

While the green card must be renewed (with a new photo and a new set of biometrics) after ten years, the residency remains valid indefinitely, provided the applicant maintains residency.

Individuals who obtained permanent residency through marriage to a U.S. citizen

**Advice of Counsel**

It is important to maintain residency because it is possible to abandon permanent resident status. Filing U.S. income tax returns, owning property in the United States, and continued physical presence in the United States are all important factors in maintaining residency—they all show intent to remain in the United States on a permanent basis.

are eligible to apply for U.S. citizenship via the naturalization process three years after the initial residency was granted.

## IV Consular Processing

If the K-3 or K-4 applicant is not in the United States or cannot file for adjustment of status for other reasons, the final green card application may be processed through IV consular processing. With IV consular processing, the applicant completes the final step of the green card process via the U.S. consulate in his or her home country or country of residence.

This process is similar to the process for obtaining K-3 and K-4 visas. After the I-130 is approved by USCIS, the case is sent to the NVC for final processing. NVC requires the applicant to submit all documentation to its office, such as marriage certificate, birth certificate, and police records for any country he or she has lived in since age sixteen. An I-864 affidavit of support must also be executed by the U.S. citizen sponsor showing his or her ability to financially support the sponsored foreign national spouse and any dependent children.

Once the NVC reviews all of the documentation, it then notifies the appropriate U.S. consulate that the applicant is ready for an interview. Applicants must also complete another medical examination with a USCIS-approved physician (similar to the one required for the K visa issuance) and the applicant and any dependent children would then be required to attend an interview at the U.S. consulate. If approved, each applicant is then issued an immigrant visa that will allow them to enter the United States as a permanent resident. Upon arrival in the United States, final processing such as fingerprinting is completed at the port of entry and a green card is mailed to each applicant.

# CHAPTER 16

# Alphabet Soup: A Summary of the More Exotic NIV Categories

## In This Chapter

➤ The A visas

➤ The E-3 visas

➤ The H-2A visas

➤ The I-1 visas

➤ The R-1 visas

Among the alphabet soup of visas, some are more popular; others are more exotic and rarely used.

# A Visas: Diplomats and Foreign Government Officials

Diplomats and foreign government officials are required to apply for A visas when traveling to the United States. A variety of A visas are available to address specific situations.

## A-1 and A-2 Visas

The A-1 visa classification is reserved for foreign nationals and their immediate family members who are entering the United States on behalf of their national government to engage solely in official activities for that government. These individuals typically hold a title such as ambassador, minister, secretary, or consul general.

The A-2 visa is for other accredited officials and employees of national governments and their immediate family members. Local government officials representing their state, province, borough, or other local political entity are not eligible for A visas.

To qualify for an A-1 or A-2 visa, the beneficiary must be performing duties that are governmental in character or nature. Governmental interest or control in a given organization is not in itself a determinative factor for the issuance of an A-1 or A-2 visa. Also, the purpose of the beneficiary's travel is critical to whether the A visa can be issued and when it should be used.

## No Petition Required

The A-1 and A-2 visas are applied for directly at the U.S. consulate; no prior petition approval is required. Consulates generally do not require A-1 visa applicants to appear for an interview; however, a consular officer can request an interview. In addition to standard visa documentation, the beneficiary must submit a diplomatic note confirming the beneficiary's status with his or her foreign government.

### Example Please

A government official traveling to the United States on official business must obtain an A visa; traveling on a visitor visa or via the Visa Waiver Program (VWP) is not permitted. A foreign official traveling to the United States to perform nongovernmental duties or to visit as a tourist does not qualify for an A visa.

Spouses and unmarried children of any age who are members of the primary beneficiary's household are considered immediate family members and may apply for A-1 classification. Those who may qualify for immediate family status on this basis include any other relative by blood, marriage, or adoption, of the primary beneficiary; a same-sex domestic partner; and a relative by blood, marriage, or adoption of the domestic partner. Domestic partners may be issued diplomatic visas if the sending government provides reciprocal treatment to domestic partners of U.S. citizens.

## A-3 Visas

Personal employees, attendants, domestic workers, or servants of A-1 visa applicants may apply for A-3 visas. For the A-3 visa to be issued, the foreign mission must have submitted the necessary prenotification of a domestic worker form to the United States Office of Protocol. This form is issued by the United States Mission to the United Nations and is attached to the diplomatic note that A-1 visa applicants are required to have for the issuance of their visa.

Unlike the primary A-1 beneficiary, the A-3 employee is required to appear at a consulate to be interviewed. A contract signed by both the A-1 employer and A-3 employee demonstrating the duties to be performed and the rate of pay is required. The contract must be in English and also in a language understood by the employee to ensure the employee understands his or her duties and rights regarding salary and working conditions. If the A-1 employer does not carry the diplomatic rank of minister or higher, or hold a position equivalent to minister or higher, the employer must demonstrate that he or she will have sufficient funds to provide fair wages and working conditions as reflected in the contract.

The consular officer also considers the number of employees the A-1 beneficiary currently employs and whether the A-1 beneficiary has reasonable ability to pay the required wage. The A-1 employer is required to pay the A-3 beneficiary's initial travel expenses to the United States or to the employee's country of normal residence at the termination of the assignment.

### Visa Vocab

A fair wage is considered to be a rate of pay at the state or federal minimum or prevailing wage (whichever is greater) for the location where the employment will occur. The prevailing wage is determined by the consular officer pursuant to the DOL's **Occupational Employment Statistics Wage Survey**.

Upon admission to the United States, A-1 and A-2 visa holders are granted duration of status (D/S) and are exempt from the US-VISIT entry-exit program. A-3 visa holders are provided an admission for three years and are subject to US-VISIT.

### Visa Vocab

US-VISIT is a security program implemented at the United States' ports of entry and is applicable for non–United States citizens between the ages of fourteen and seventy-nine. Upon entry, the officer scans biometrics, or fingerprints, and takes a digital photograph of the applicant. Visitors admitted on the following visas are exempt from US-VISIT:

➤ A-1and A-2 visas

➤ C-3 visas

➤ G-1, G-2, G-3, G-4 visas

➤ NATO-1, NATO-2, NATO-3, NATO-4, NATO-5, NATO-6 visas

# E-3 Visas: Australian Specialty Occupation Professional

The E-3 classification is for Australian citizens coming to the United States to perform services in a specialty occupation. As with the H-1B visa, a specialty occupation requires theoretical and practical application of a body of knowledge in professional fields and a bachelor's degree, or its equivalent, as minimum requirements.

Besides possessing the necessary academic or other qualifying credentials for the specialty occupation, the E-3 visa beneficiary must have a legitimate offer of employment in the United States in a position that qualifies as a specialty occupation.

## LCA Requirement

Also like the H-1B classification, the E-3 classification requires the petitioner to submit an ETA-9035 labor condition application (LCA) form with the DOL. The LCA outlines the details and terms of the employment, including salary and job location.

Once the LCA has been certified by DOL, the beneficiary is eligible to apply for an E-3 visa directly at a U.S. consulate. The beneficiary must have the required DS-160 visa application form along with the certified LCA and should also present academic or other credentials demonstrating his or her qualifications for the position. Finally, a job offer letter or other documentation from the employer should be presented to establish the details of the specialty position in the United States and that the beneficiary will be paid the higher of the actual or prevailing wage stated on the LCA.

A beneficiary in the United States who seeks to change status to E-3 (or to extend current E-3 status) may use the I-129 petition for nonimmigrant workers to apply for the status change or extension. When the petition is approved, a I-797 notice of approval will be issued. Should the beneficiary plan to travel outside of the United States, he or she will be required to apply for an E-3 visa at a U.S. consulate abroad.

The initial period of stay and subsequent extensions of stay may be granted for up to two years. An E-3 beneficiary's spouse and unmarried children under twenty-one years of age are entitled to the same E-3 classification.

# H-2A Visas: Temporary Agricultural Worker

The H-2A program allows U.S. employers to bring foreign nationals to the United States to fill temporary agricultural jobs for which U.S. workers are not available.

To qualify for H-2A nonimmigrant classification, the job offered must be of a temporary or seasonal nature, and the employer must demonstrate that there are not enough U.S. workers who are able, willing, qualified, or available to perform the temporary work. The employer must also show that the employment of H-2A workers will not adversely affect the wages and working conditions of similarly employed U.S. workers.

H-2A petitions may be approved only for nationals of countries that DHS has designated as eligible to participate in the H-2A program. The list of H-2A-eligible countries is published in a notice in the Federal Register (FR) by DHS on a rolling basis. A national from a country not on the list may be the beneficiary of an approved H-2A petition only if the DHS determines that it is in the United States' interest.

### Advice of Counsel

E-3 spouses may apply for work authorization to work in the United States, but E-3 dependent children may not.

### Advice of Counsel

A petitioner, agent, facilitator, recruiter, or similar employment service is prohibited from collecting a job placement fee or other compensation, either directly or indirectly, at any time from an H-2A worker as a condition of employment.

## *Labor Certification*

The petition process begins with the employer submitting the ETA-9035 (LCA) form to the DOL. Once the LCA is certified, the employer must submit it and the I-129 form to USCIS. Once the I-129 is approved, prospective H-2A workers who are outside of the United States may apply for the H-2A visa at a U.S. consulate abroad.

Generally, USCIS may grant H-2A classification for the period of time authorized on the temporary labor certification, which is usually no longer than one year as the employment is intended to be temporary and/or seasonal. H-2A classification may be extended for qualifying employment in increments of up to one year for a maximum period of three years. Once a worker has held H-2A nonimmigrant status for three years, he or she is required to leave and remain outside the United States for an uninterrupted period of at least three months before seeking readmission as an H-2A nonimmigrant.

Spouses and unmarried children under twenty-one years of age of H-2A workers may seek admission to the United States through H-4 nonimmigrant classification, but they may not engage in employment in the United States.

## *Reporting Requirements*

Once an H-2A worker enters the United States, certain changes in his or her employment must be reported to USCIS (check the USCIS website—www.USCIS.gov—for the most up-to-date reporting address). Petitioners of H-2A workers must notify USCIS within two workdays if the worker:

> ➤ fails to report to work within five workdays of the employment start date on the H-2A petition or within five workdays of the start date established by the petitioner, whichever is later;

> ➤ fails to report for work for a period of five consecutive workdays without the consent of the employer;

> ➤ is terminated prior to the completion of agricultural labor or services for which he or she was hired; or

> ➤ completes the agricultural labor or services for which he or she was hired more than thirty days earlier than the date specified in the H-2A petition.

# I-1 Visa: Representatives of Foreign Media

The I-1 visa is for professionals who represent foreign press, radio, film, or other foreign media outlets. This includes primary employees of foreign information media engaged in filming news events or documentaries and employees of independent production companies if the employee holds a credential issued by a professional journalistic association.

Uncredentialed foreign media representatives may qualify for I visas and satisfy the definition of "foreign media representative" if the sending country does not have a credentialing authority, or where the credentialing authority does not have jurisdiction over the class of journalists to which the beneficiary belongs.

To qualify for the I-1 visa, the beneficiary must be coming to the United States to engage in this profession and have a home office in a foreign country. As a representative of foreign media, the beneficiary cannot travel to the United States and engage in his or her profession without an I-1 nonimmigrant visa, even if he or she is a citizen of a country that participates in the Visa Waiver Program. There are limited instances under which a media representative may be eligible to travel with a B visitor's visa.

## The I Visa Process

The beneficiary applies directly at a U.S. consulate for the I-1 visa (no I-129 petition is required), and the consular officer determines whether an activity in the United States qualifies for the issuance of the visa. With the required visa documentation, the beneficiary should provide proof of the intended employment appropriate for the position type such as:

➤ Staff journalist: A letter from the employer detailing the position held within the company, the journalist's qualifications, and purpose and length of stay in the United States

➤ Freelance journalist under contract to a media organization: A copy of the contract with the organization that shows the employee's name, the position held within the company, the purpose and length of stay in the United States, and the duration of contract

➤ Independent production company under contract to a media organization: A letter from the organization commissioning the work providing a description of the program being filmed, the period of time required for filming in the United States, and the duration of the contract

The validity period of the visa is based upon the reciprocity agreements between the United States and the beneficiary's home country. At the port of entry, the period of admission is for D/S; the I visa holder is considered to be maintaining status in the United States provided he or she is engaged in the vocation for which the visa was issued.

Spouses and children under the age of twenty-one of I-1 visa holders are eligible to apply for I visas to accompany the beneficiary to the United States for the duration of the assignment.

# R-1 Visa: Temporary Nonimmigrant Religious Workers

The R-1 category is reserved for workers who will be employed by a nonprofit religious organization or an organization that is affiliated with a religious denomination to work at least part-time (twenty hours per week) as one of the following:

> ➤ A minister

> ➤ A person working in a professional capacity in a religious vocation or occupation

> ➤ A person working for a religious organization in a religious vocation and who for two years immediately preceding the R-1 petition has been a member of a religious denomination with a bona fide nonprofit religious organization in the United States

### Visa Vocab

In order to determine what is considered a bona fide religious denomination, USCIS considers whether the denomination has established places of religious worship and religious congregations, has religious services and ceremonies, has the presence of an ecclesiastical government and a recognized creed and form of worship.

When filing an I-129 form on behalf of the R-1 beneficiary, the following supporting evidence should be provided by the petitioner in regard to the petitioning religious organization and the beneficiary:

> ➤ Evidence that the petitioner has tax-exempt status such as a copy of a current, valid individual IRS 501(c)(3) letter. If the petitioner is recognized as tax-exempt under a group tax exemption, a copy of the group ruling should be provided.

> ➤ Evidence of the intended compensation for the beneficiary (salaried or unsalaried), such as budgets showing monies set aside for salaries and/or evidence that room and board will be provided.

If the beneficiary will be self-supporting, evidence must be provided to show:

> ➤ The beneficiary has been accepted into a temporary, traditionally uncompensated missionary program and an explanation of the duties associated with the missionary work has been offered

➤ The beneficiary's intended position is part of an established program for temporary uncompensated missionary work that is part of a broader international program of missionary work sponsored by the denomination

➤ The petitioner has an established program for temporary uncompensated missionary work in which foreign workers have previously participated in R-1 status, have traditionally been uncompensated, and have been given formal training. Participation in such missionary work must be an established element of religious development in that denomination.

➤ Evidence establishing the organization's religious denomination maintains missionary programs in the United States and abroad

➤ Evidence of the beneficiary's sources of self-support, such as personal bank records, family savings, room and board with the United States host families, and donations from the denomination's churches

The beneficiary should supply evidence of membership in a religious denomination having a bona fide nonprofit religious organization in the United States for at least two years immediately preceding the filing of form I-129.

If the beneficiary will be working as a minister in the United States, this evidence should include:

➤ A copy of the beneficiary's certificate of ordination or similar documents

➤ Documents reflecting acceptance of the beneficiary's qualification as a minister in the religious denomination, as well as evidence of completion of any course of prescribed theological education at an accredited theological institution (transcripts, degree), and documentation that establishes that the theological institution is accredited by the denomination

➤ If the denomination does not require a specific theological education, evidence of the denomination's requirements for ordination to minister should be provided, as well as details on the duties performed by virtue of ordination, the denomination's levels of ordination, and evidence of the beneficiary's completion of the denomination's requirements for ordination.

When filing the I-129 form, the petitioner may request an initial period of stay for up to thirty months. Extensions of R-1 status may be granted for up to an additional thirty months. The maximum period of stay in R-1 status is sixty months (five years); however, if the beneficiary's employment in the United States was less than six months and the beneficiary did not live continually in the United States, or if the beneficiary lives outside of the United States and commutes to the United States, the five-year limitation does not apply.

Spouses and unmarried children under twenty-one years of age of R-1 workers may seek admission via R-2 nonimmigrant classification. R-2 visa holders may not engage in employment in the United States.

# PART FIVE

# Common NIV Issues

# CHAPTER 17

## The Visa Waiver Program

### In This Chapter

➤ Traveling visa-free

➤ Eligibility requirements

➤ Length of stay

As you may have concluded by now, obtaining a nonimmigrant visa can be confusing, time-consuming, and bureaucratic. And yet foreign travelers come to the United States by the thousands every day to visit Disney World, engage in business meetings in New York or Los Angeles, or visit friends or relatives who live in the States.

How is this possible? Do all of these visitors have to obtain visas?

## Visa-Free Travel

Just as almost any American citizen can get on a plane and fly to London or Tokyo on vacation or for business without obtaining a foreign visa, residents of most European and several Asian countries can travel to America without going through the sometimes grueling exercise of obtaining a visa in their passports.

They are able to do so thanks to the Visa Waiver Program. Without the Visa Waiver Program, travel into the United States would effectively

### Visa Vocab

The Visa Waiver Program (VWP) permits nationals of certain specified countries to travel to the United States without a visa.

grind to a halt because millions of European and Asian visitors would have to obtain an NIV to enter the United States. Fortunately, this is not the case.

As the name suggests, under the VWP the U.S. government waives the requirement for foreign nationals of certain countries to obtain a visa if the trip is short-term in nature.

## *Eligible Countries*

Specifically, the VWP permits nationals of thirty-six countries to travel to the United States for periods of less than ninety days for business or pleasure without having to obtain a visa. The thirty-six countries that this applies to are:

➤ Andorra

➤ Australia

➤ Austria

➤ Belgium

➤ Brunei

➤ Czech Republic

➤ Denmark

➤ Estonia

➤ Finland

➤ France

➤ Greece

➤ Hungary

➤ Iceland

➤ Ireland

➤ Italy

➤ Japan

➤ Latvia

➤ Liechtenstein

➤ Lithuania

➤ Luxembourg

➤ Malta

➤ Monaco

➤ Norway

➤ Portugal

➤ San Marino

➤ Singapore

➤ Slovakia

➤ Slovenia

➤ South Korea

➤ Spain

➤ Sweden

➤ Switzerland

➤ Netherlands

➤ United Kingdom

# Qualifications

To take advantage of the VWP, a foreign national must meet a few basic eligibility requirements.

## Machine-Readable Passport

Applicants must have a valid machine-readable passport with an expiration date at least six months past their expected stay in the United States. How do you know if your passport is machine readable?

### Advice of Counsel

Nation-specific passport requirements may also apply—check the DOS's website before attempting to travel!

A machine-readable passport is one that has biographical data entered on the picture page at the bottom, so it can be swiped through an electronic passport reader. Here's what it looks like:

## ESTA

Applicants must register with the Electronic System for Travel Authorization (ESTA). ESTA is a preclearance system whereby the individual submits basic biographical information (name, DOB, passport number) either through an online website (https://esta. cbp.dhs. gov/) or at a kiosk at an airport. Either way, the applicant receives an ESTA approval that then gets submitted to either the airport official, Transportation Security Administration (TSA)—or whomever else requests it.

## Return Plane Ticket

Applicants traveling by plane must have a return plane ticket.

## Immigrant Intent

Applicants must be able to demonstrate that they have sufficient funds to support themselves while in the United States and do not have immigrant intent—an absolute no-no for using the VWP.

## Business or Pleasure

The purpose of the individual's visit to the United States must be for either business or for pleasure—just as with a B visa.

### Advice of Counsel

Travel by private aircraft is not permitted under the VWP—only commercial air travel meets the VWP requirement. Those traveling in private jets are required to obtain some other NIV, such as a B-1.

With respect to tourism, the basis for entry under the VWP is pretty clear-cut. A tourist is a tourist—whether visiting friends, touring the Grand Canyon, or seeing a show in Vegas.

With respect to business, however, the rules are less clear (just as with the B-1). The bright line rules are that the individual cannot receive direct remuneration from a U.S. employer while in the United States nor engage in productive work.

As with the B visa, however, the devil is in the details. Is a senior business executive entering the United States to conduct negotiations in Chicago considered to be working in the United States? What about a technical engineer supervising repair work on an assembly line? In both cases, these are in all likelihood permitted activities that do not constitute *work*—but admittedly the test is somewhat subjective. Hence, it's important to be specific when explaining the purpose of the trip to a U.S. inspector as well as to carry corroborating documents such as a letter from the employer as to the exact nature of the trip.

If the applicant satisfies the above requirements, the necessity to obtain a visa is waived—hence the name Visa Waiver Program.

### Advice of Counsel

The same basic test for immigrant intent applies to both VWP visitors and B visa applicants.

### Advice of Counsel

Technically, the bases for entry to the United States via the VWP are identical to those for obtaining a B-1 or B-2 visa, and the same restrictions apply.

### Advice of Counsel

See chapter 7 for more information on issues relating to entering the United States for business under a B-1 visa. The same rules generally apply when entering the United States under the VWP.

The waiver concept works in both directions, however. Once someone enters on the VWP he or she also waives any rights to extend the stay, to change the purpose of the trip, or to change status. What does this mean?

# Permitted Stay

Applicants may be admitted to the United States for up to ninety days—and no longer. The "up to" part is also important. The exact duration given to the applicant is determined by the immigration inspector.

The ninety-day period is not renewable or extendable—in other words, when your ninety days are up, you have to leave. And the government really means it. There are rare and unique circumstances when the ninety-day period may be extended, but they relate to exigent circumstances—you have been admitted to the hospital, you are in jail, etc. Any other reason—you are having a really good time on vacation, you missed your flight, etc.— is a nonstarter. For all practical purposes, if you enter on the VWP you can pretty much guarantee that your ninety days (or whatever time period you might be given) is a hard-and-fast, nonnegotiable deadline.

### Advice of Counsel

The Visa Waiver Program permits entries of up to ninety days—but no more. The exact amount of time granted is shown on the I-94W card, which is issued by an immigration inspector when the applicant enters the United States.

## *The Green I-94W Card*

Upon entry to the United States, the applicant fills out a green I-94W card. This is not a green card. The I-94W card, with the *W* standing for "waiver," functions and looks exactly like a regular I-94 card except that it is green rather than white. (As a reminder, NIV holders complete a white I-94 card.) The I-94W card governs your status when you enter under the VWP.

The I-94W card looks like this:

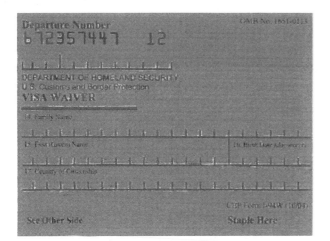

### Advice of Counsel

A green I-94W card is not a green card. Airline officials (who pass out the cards) sometimes confuse the two, asking passengers if they need the green card as a foreign visitor when entering the United States. Don't be fooled.

At inspection, the officer stamps the green I-94W card with a date—that is the date you are entitled to remain legally in the United States pursuant to the VWP. Usually that date is ninety days from the date of entry—it will not be longer (unless in error).

## Status

By using the VWP, you are waiving the right to change your status. For example, suppose you are a French citizen waiting in Paris for your L-1 (intracompany transferee) visa to be issued by the consulate.

When you receive it, you intend to begin a one-year assignment working in New York. The L-1 visa is taking longer than you would like, though, and you need to get to New York to get your life sorted out—rent an apartment, buy a car, etc. Can you come early to New York on the VWP and then switch over to your L visa? No.

You can go to New York to do all the things described above under the VWP, but once your ninety days are up, you have to leave. There is no method of simply changing your status from VW to L-1, or any other NIV category for that matter. You waived that right by using the VWP.

So in the example above you could go to New York and get organized, but then you would have to return to France, obtain your L-1 visa, and reenter the United States to activate your L status.

### *How Often Can I Go to the United States?*

A question that often comes up is whether the VWP can be used over and over again? The answer is yes—but.

Technically, there is no limit to the number of times an individual is permitted to use the VWP. In other words, someone traveling on business to the United States to conduct a lengthy transaction might fly in and out of New York once a week for several months in a row. That is permitted.

But every time an individual enters the United States on the VWP, the CBP inspector asks what he or she is doing, and the applicant has to overcome the intending immigrant presumption.

**Advice of Counsel**

Dual intent is not permitted under the VWP.

If that individual has made, say, five trips to the United States one right after the other, and each trip was over sixty days in length, it may seem to an inspector as if the person is actually working in the United States.

By the same token, if a tourist repeatedly travels to the United States in ninety-day intervals, it raises a reasonable presumption as to what the individual is actually doing—and whether he or she may be working illegally. Therefore, while there is no technical legal limit to using the VWP, there may be a practical limit. Overuse of the VWP, while not prohibited, may in fact cause an immigration inspector to deny entry (or threaten to do so in the future) if repeated use of the VWP creates suspicion.

# VWP vs B Visa

As mentioned above, the bases for entry to the United States under the VWP is the same as those of a B visa. So why would anyone from a visa waiver country bother to get a B visa? There are a few reasons.

The individual might anticipate numerous trips in and out of the United States over a protracted period of time. In that case, the B visa may give an additional level of comfort insofar as the applicant will get somewhat less scrutiny from the inspector with a B visa than under the VWP.

A B visa might also be appropriate when an individual anticipates remaining in the United States for longer than ninety days such as when a person is seeking medical treatment that might take four or five months.

For the ordinary tourist or business traveler who is eligible to travel on the VWP, obtaining a B visa is generally unnecessary. In certain circumstances, however, it might still make sense.

It's important to keep in mind that the VWP is a privilege, and like all privileges it can be revoked. If an individual is denied entry on the VWP for some reason (say, repeated use noted above), or if the individual has a criminal background or other issues, the government will deny entry under the VWP. This does not mean that the individual is prohibited from coming to the United States—it simply means that the privilege of doing so without needing to get a visa is revoked, and the individual will have to obtain a visa to do so.

# CHAPTER 18

# Changing Your Status

As you have no doubt concluded by now, in addition to being complex and bureaucratic, the U.S. visa system is also not exactly a model of flexibility. Visas are issued to specific individuals for specific purposes and subject to specific limitations. Failure to comply with the terms of a particular visa can result in the visa becoming invalid.

So what happens when circumstances change? For example, what if you lose your job or want to start a new job? What do you do then?

Suppose, for example, you entered the United States with a B-1 visitor's visa to engage in business negotiations in Miami. While you were there, you were offered a job. As you know (having read this book), those with B status are not permitted to engage in employment while in the United States. To begin work you need a new status—one that permits you to work.

In other words, you need to change your status.

**Advice of Counsel**

Remember, when you are in the United States it is your status that determines what you are permitted—or forbidden—to do; it is not your visa stamp. Therefore, to engage in a new activity you need to acquire a new status. This may or may not require that you get a new visa as you will see later in this chapter.

# Two Ways to Change Status

How do you change your status? You have two options.

### Get a New Visa

One way to change your status is simply to leave the United States and obtain a new visa. Once you enter the United States with whatever new visa you have, you automatically activate your new status. Recall that status only exists once you are physically in the United States. Once you leave, your old status disappears. When you reenter with a new visa, your new status begins.

When you return to the United States, the government looks at your eligibility to enter on the new visa as if you were starting from scratch. It doesn't matter that you were offered a job in the United States that you really want or that you had already been granted a B visa, as in the example above. Such reasoning is irrelevant to the issue of whether you are entitled to a new visa.

### Advice of Counsel

As opposed to requesting an extension of status in the same category, where you are simply asking for more time in the same status, changing status by obtaining a new visa essentially means starting the process of petition approval and application at a consulate all over again.

Leaving the United States and obtaining a new visa, reentering the United States with the new visa and thus acquiring a new status is the cleanest and conceptually simplest manner of changing one's status. However, in real life the mechanics and timing of doing this can be a hassle.

What if you don't want to leave the United States or circumstances make it difficult to do so? What do you do then? Or to put the question differently, how do you change your status without obtaining a new visa?

### Change Your Status, Not Your Visa

Foreign visitors in this situation often say, "I came in with a B visa, but now I want to work. So I need a new visa."

As you have learned by now, this statement is both right and wrong. It is right in that you do need a new visa if you leave the United States and wish to reenter with a visa appropriate to your new situation. But it is wrong in that all you may need is a new status.

### Advice of Counsel

You may have several different visa stamps in your passport. For example, a B-1 business visitor visa as well as an H-1B visa. Is this OK? Generally yes, but unless the government cancels your visa (by stamping it as such), you need to be very clear when you enter the United States which visa stamp you want to use to be admitted.

## Change of Status Process

If you leave the United States and reenter with a new visa, the problem is self-correcting. Your status is changed by virtue of your departure and reentry.

But a second and easier way to change status is by filing a change of status petition with USCIS. This can be done both for the principal foreign national and his or her family members.

### Visa Vocab

A change of status petition is a filing made with USCIS that requests the government to grant new status. The requirements for obtaining the new status are not made any more or less stringent than leaving the United States and applying for a new visa.

The filing requirements and forms for a change of status petition are substantially the same as if you were outside the United States and requesting USCIS to issue you an approved petition for the first time. The only difference is how you answer the second question in part 2 of the I-129 form.

---

**Part 2. Information About This Petition** *(See instructions for fee information.)*

1. **Requested Nonimmigrant Classification** *(Write classification symbol):* [                    ]

2. **Basis for Classification** *(Check one):*

   ☑ **a.** New employment.

   ☐ **b.** Continuation of previously approved employment without change with the same employer.

   ☐ **c.** Change in previously approved employment.

   ☐ **d.** New concurrent employment.

   ☐ **e.** Change of employer.

   ☐ **f.** Amended petition.

3. Provide the most recent petition/application receipt number for the beneficiary. If none exists, indicate "N/A."

   [                                                        ]

4. **Requested Action** *(Check one):*

   ☐ **a.** Notify the office in **Part 4** so each beneficiary can obtain a visa or be admitted. (**NOTE:** *A petition is not required for an E-1, E-2, H-1B1 Chile/Singapore, or TN visa.*)

   ☑ **b.** Change each beneficiary's status and extend their stay since he, she, or they are all now in the U.S. in another status *(see instructions for limitations)*. This is available only where you check "New Employment" in **Item 2**, above.

   ☐ **c.** Extend the stay of each beneficiary since he, she, or they now hold this status.

   ☐ **d.** Amend the stay of each beneficiary since he, she, or they now hold this status.

   ☐ **e.** Extend the status of a nonimmigrant classification based on a Free Trade Agreement. *(See Free Trade Supplement for TN and H1B1 to Form I-129.)*

   ☐ **f.** Change status to a nonimmigrant classification based on a Free Trade Agreement. *(See Free Trade Supplement for TN and H1B1 to Form I-129.)*

5. **Total number of workers in petition** *(See instructions relating to when more than one worker can be included.):* [          ]

Form I-129 (Rev. 01/19/11)Y Page 2

---

## Example Please

If you were switching from B status to H-1B status, you would tick box A, New Employment, of question 2, Basis for Classification. As you can see in question 4, Requested Action, on the form, you are asking the government to change each beneficiary's status and extend their stay since he, she, or they are all now in the United States in another status. In this example you are requesting new employment because your current status (B) does not permit employment. This would also hold true even if you had one type of employment status (L-1A) and were switching to another type of employment status (H-1B).

Assuming you qualify for a change of status, when USCIS approves your case it will issue you an I-797 form with a new I-94 card showing your new status at the bottom. Your old I-94 card is then technically void. The government has now given you a new and different status—and you didn't have to leave the country.

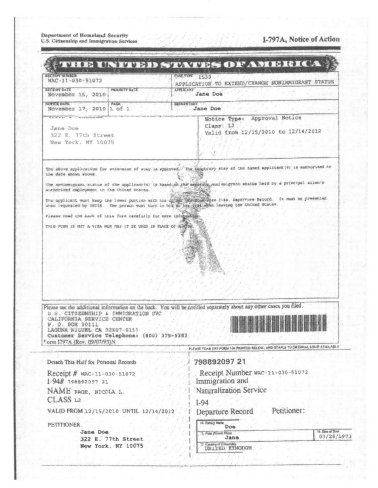

# When You Might Not Want to Change Your Status

When USCIS issues you a new I-94 card, it has changed your status, your legal purpose for being in the United States. What USCIS has not done (and for that matter, cannot do) is amend your visa. As long as you remain in the United States and your status is current, you are fine. The moment you leave the United States, however, you have no basis to reenter the United States because your visa isn't current. You need a new visa.

To get a new visa, you have to use your USCIS I-797 change of status approval notice to apply at a consulate to obtain a new visa, just like any other applicant.

But if you are in the United States in one status (say, B) and you want another status (say, L-1), you are not necessarily required to file a change of status application; you could simply obtain a new approved petition.

It is a question of tactics. You could, in the above example, ask the USCIS to grant you an approved petition (or an initial issuance, as if it were your first filing), rather than request a change of status. Why would you do this?

You would do this because an initial issuance might be reviewed somewhat less stringently in some nonimmigrant visa categories than would a change of status petition. This is tricky, however, so you would need to talk to your counsel to determine if this applies to you.

And in cases where individuals are required to travel abroad frequently—or where the individual's visa may be near expiration—it might be simpler to apply for an approved petition, obtain the visa stamp, and reenter the United States than it would be to file for a change of status.

## Considering a New Job Offer

You might not want to file a change of status application if you are on the fence as to whether to accept a new job. After all, relocating to the United States entails a number of complex personal decisions—finances, family, and long-term happiness among them. These are made ever more fraught when you don't yet have a visa in hand.

### Advice of Counsel

Bear in mind you lose nothing by applying for an initial issuance, other than time and expense. Applying for and receiving an initial issuance (meaning a filing without asking for a change of status) simply means that USCIS has concluded that you have met the criteria for a basic visa category. Put differently, it's just a piece of paper (albeit a valuable one if you choose to apply for the visa). By itself, it has no impact on your status.

In this case, you might want to get the visa petition approved before you commit to a particular job—but without monkeying with your status. After all, what happens if you commit to the new job and the case is denied or delayed? An approved petition allows you to have the comfort of knowing you can apply for a visa at your leisure, without affecting your underlying status. After all, you don't have to apply for the visa—you simply can. You can put the approved petition on the shelf while you think about it, or even throw it away—the government is not going to care. Having an approved petition certainly gives a greater peace of mind when weighing all your options.

### Travel Considerations

You might apply for an initial issuance rather than a change of status—and this is the more common case—if you know you will be traveling out of the United States between the time you file for a change of status and the time you think USCIS might approve your case (say, three to six months). Remember, you only have status once you are in the United States—when you leave, it disappears. So if you apply for a change of status and then leave the United States, you don't have any status to change. For this reason, if you file and then leave, the government will treat your case as having been abandoned.

Thus if your travel schedule is such that you are likely to need to leave the United States after you file a change of status case but before USCIS approves it, you might as well simply get an initial issuance and put it in your back pocket so that you can obtain a visa at your leisure.

# Who Qualifies for a Change in Status?

To qualify for a change of status, you must meet the following criteria:

➤ You entered the United States (legally) in a nonimmigrant category

➤ You are in status

➤ The government likes you

Let's take each in turn.

### Are You an NIV?

First, you must have entered the United States (legally) in a nonimmigrant category. The requirement that you entered the United States legally (meaning that you were inspected by an immigration officer) is in a sense obvious. If you came in illegally, you have no status, and therefore you have no status to change.

Similarly, you have to be in a nonimmigrant category. You cannot change your status if you entered under visa waiver, as a green card holder, or as a U.S. citizen. Strange as it may seem, situations do arise where someone enters the United States in one category (say, as a green card holder) and wants to change to an NIV category. No dice. Only a nonimmigrant can change to another nonimmigrant status.

## Are You in Status?

This leads to the second requirement, and this is absolutely critical—you have to be in a legal status to change your status. Suppose you did come into the United States legally, but you overstayed the date on your I-94 card. You are out of status.

If you are out of status, USCIS will not—I repeat, will not—change your status, except under extraordinary and exigent circumstances—and sometimes, not even then. The reason that you might be out of status—you forgot, your job kept you here longer, your wife left you— are in the view of the government totally irrelevant. Simply put, the government does not care. In its view, you and you alone are responsible for maintaining and preserving your status.

### Advice of Counsel

In our experience, the only circumstances that constitute extraordinary and exigent circumstances that might permit the government to overlook your being out of status (and grant you a change of status) are medical emergencies and government error.

## Does the Government Like You?

The last requirement for a change of status is for the government to like you. What does this mean? First, it means that you have not overstayed the expiration of your status for more than six months. If you have overstayed, you are then subject to the statutory bar and USCIS is not going to change your status, no matter what.

It also means that there is no subjective factor in your case that leads USCIS to conclude that it simply doesn't want to change your status. Or put differently, you don't have something in your past or the reason for your request that raises a red flag.

Bear in mind that it is entirely in the discretion of USCIS to change your status. If the case looks suspicious or problematic, USCIS will simply deny the request. Problematic cases that can lead to denial are:

> ➤ Changing status from B (tourist) to F-1 (student), unless the basis for the B visa was to check out a particular school.

> ➤ Changing status from L or H to B, which often occurs when an individual loses his or her job or simply runs out of time. USCIS is generally not sympathetic

to granting someone with L or H status more time after the end of a permitted employment period.

➤ Changing status from H-1B to L-1. Time spent in one category is aggregated toward the other. For example, an individual who has been in the United States for five years in L status will only be eligible (assuming he or she is eligible) for one year in H status.

## Advice of Counsel

If you are out of status, USCIS will almost never change your status; although, if you otherwise qualify for the new visa category, USCIS may approve the petition and tell you to apply abroad for the visa.

Now, the fact that you may be ineligible for a change of status does not mean you are not eligible for the NIV category itself. The government might easily conclude that you meet the basic criteria for the visa (say, an L-1B) but that because you are out of status for some reason, you are ineligible for a change of status. That does not mean you are ineligible for that visa category as a whole.

In that case, USCIS would issue you an approved petition but no new I-94 card. This is just as if you had requested an initial issuance. You would then have to leave the United States and reenter with a visa to get the new status.

How does the government know whether you are or are not in status when you file to change your status? Simple—you have to include a copy of your current I-94 card with the filing. You must also complete several forms that ask for your current I-94 details (date of entry and expiration). Provided that you file the case on the day prior to the expiration of your I-94 card, you are in status and thus eligible for a change of status.

Of course, you could be in violation of status even if you file before the expiration date on your I-94 card. The classic example is if you are waiting tables while in the United States on a B visa. You are then out of status due to your conduct. Will the government generally be aware that you have violated your status, other than the date on your I-94 card? Frankly, no. Unless you have done something such as lie to an immigration inspector or been arrested, the fact that you may technically not be in status due to your action is difficult for the government to know.

# Who Doesn't Qualify for Change of Status?

Certain individuals do not qualify for a change of status—no ifs, ands, or buts. On the top of the list is anyone who entered the United States under visa waiver. One of the things you waive is the right to request a change or extension of your status.

In addition, the regulations provide that people holding a visa in the following nonimmigrant visa categories are not eligible to change to another category or extend their status:

> ➤ C (aliens in transit)

> ➤ D (crewmen)

> ➤ K-1 or K-2 (fiancé(e) or dependent of fiancé(e))

> ➤ S (witness or informant)

> ➤ TWOV (transit without visa)

The following nonimmigrant visa categories have restrictions about when you can change your status:

> ➤ J-1 (exchange visitor). If you are subject to the two-year foreign residence requirement, you cannot change status, with certain exceptions.

> ➤ M-1 (vocational student). You cannot change status to F-1 and you cannot change status to H-1B if the vocational training helped you qualify for the H classification.

# What Happens After You File

Suppose you meet the eligibility requirements and you file a petition to change your status. What happens then?

First, provided that you are in status when you filed (meaning, in large part, that your I-94 card was still valid when you mailed in the petition), you are legal to remain in the United States during the time the government takes to adjudicate your case—even if that is a very long time.

On the other hand, you are not eligible to begin working until such time as your case is approved, if you are switching from a nonemployment-type visa to an employment visa. (There is one exception to this: if you are switching from H-1B from employer X to H-1B from employer Y—see chapter 8).

If, for example, you file a change of status from B to H-1B, you may begin working on the date USCIS approves your petition and changes your status—but not before. Similarly, a person can't begin attending school under a student visa (F or M) before the change of status is approved.

## What is Your Status?

What is your status while you're waiting for the government to approve your case? After all, your status may have expired—and it absolutely has if your I-94 card has expired. But the government has not acted to change your status, and therefore you do not technically have status.

The answer is that you are in a nebulous category called lawfully present (LP). For our purposes the distinction between LP and status is not important. What matters is that you are legal in the United States while the case is pending—until the government makes a decision on the case. If the case is approved, all is generally well and you are retroactively deemed in status during the period the government reviewed your case.

On the other hand, should your case be denied you are immediately deemed out of status. The government will issue a notice of denial, which will indicate when you are required to leave the United States. USCIS also dates the period you were out of status from the time your original I-94 card expired, which could have been many, many months before you received a final decision on your case. The length of time you have been out of status in the United States can have ramifications on whether or not you are eligible to apply for another visa in the future.

As a final point, status is specific and unique to each individual. Consequently, each individual must act to change his or her status if required. If the principal individual successfully acts to change status (from B to H-1B, say) but his wife and kids do not, they can end up out of status. This can and often does create quite a mess.

# CHAPTER 19

# The Difference Between an Amendment and a Change of Status

---

## In This Chapter

➤ The difference between an amendment and a change of status

➤ When amendments are required

➤ Eligibility

---

In the last chapter we discussed changing your nonimmigrant status from one category to another, from B-1 to H-1B or vice versa, for example. These are cases where the alphabetical category you desire is different from the one you happen to be in.

Another situation may arise where you may want to change the circumstances of your status within the same alphabetical category. This is known as an amendment of status.

## Same Status, Different Circumstances

All nonimmigrant employment visas are employer specific. If you have a valid H-1B for company A, but company B wants to hire you, you will need a new H-1B status to work for company B. You are not seeking a new status, at least not in the sense

### Visa Vocab

An amendment of status petition requests USCIS to amend your status to reflect changes in your situation within the same NIV category.

of a new alphabetical category. Your status will still be H-1B, whether you are working for company A or for company B. So you don't want or need a change of status.

## Job Changes

In addition to being needed when changing employers, amendment of status applications are required when a job changes dramatically. The nature of the job is critical to most employment-based NIVs. For example, an H-1B job must be professional; an L-1A position must be managerial or executive in nature. USCIS approves your case after it has reviewed the underlying job and found that it meets the requirements for that type of visa.

If you're holding the Chief Operating Officer position (an executive position for L-1A purposes) and your job was changed to that of Chief Financial Officer or Head of Business Development, which may also be considered executive or managerial, you may still qualify for L-1A status—but that is a decision made by USCIS. The positions of Chief Financial Officer or Head of Business Development were not the positions that USCIS approved when it initially approved your case. So in certain circumstances you must ask USCIS to amend your status, even when working for the same employer in the same status.

## Corporate Changes

An amendment of status might be necessary if your employer undergoes a corporate restructuring such as a merger or acquisition. For example, you might have an E (investor) visa to work for a German-owned company. As discussed in chapter 10, if the foreign company you work for is sold to any company that is not mostly German owned, your E visa will be imperiled.

### Advice of Counsel

Corporate name changes generally do not require an amendment of status. That being said, employees in such circumstances frequently want to obtain a new visa stamp given that the name change may confuse immigration officials and cause delays when entering the United States.

Similarly, suppose you were an intercompany transferee on an L-1A visa. You were transferred from the Japanese parent company to its U.S. subsidiary. What happens if the U.S. subsidiary is sold to or merges with another company or even changes its name?

In each of the above examples, your status may not technically change—in fact, the corporate change may not have any direct impact on your job at all—but you might have to ask USCIS to amend your status.

# Requirements for Filing an Amendment of Status

Each specific nonimmigrant category has rules particular to itself. Let's discuss some in turn.

## B Visa

The easiest to understand is the B visa. Although the criteria for a B-1 and B-2 visa are different, they are so broad and they overlap so much that you will almost never need to amend your status from one to the other. If you enter the United States on a B-1 visa to discuss business but end up taking a side trip to Vegas, you are fine. Don't bother the government with an amendment of status petition. And vice versa if you came to see Vegas and ended up talking business in the casino, you don't need to file a petition.

## H-1B Visa—Material Changes in Employment

The H-1B (professional worker) visa is perhaps the best known and most common nonimmigrant employment visa. Consequently, a body of law and rules has been built around it when changes in employment require an amendment to be filed.

A new petition must be filed when there are substantial changes to the individual's employment. The following are specific examples of what the government believes constitute such substantial changes:

> ➤ The location of the individual's employment moves outside of the metropolitan area of employment shown on the I-129 petition (for example, from Chicago to Miami)

> ➤ There is a significant change in the individual's duties from one specialty occupation to another

> ➤ There is a material change in the terms and conditions of employment

> ➤ A new labor condition application (LCA) is required to be filed

An amended petition is not required for promotions within the same general job category. And the government has stated that minor changes—in either job duties or salary—do not require an amended petition. Whether a change is minor or material is not very helpfully spelled out, however.

But then how will the government know if an individual's terms of employment have changed? The short answer is it won't. All an immigration inspector sees is a valid I-94 card and visa. Beyond that, the inspector simply does not look very deep into the bona fides of the underlying petition. For this reason, many employers do not take any action to file a new petition based on minor variations or modifications to an employee's job description.

On the other hand, changes from one job category to another (engineer to programmer, for example) generally do warrant a new petition, and many employers file amended petitions in these cases.

Ultimately each case must be looked at on its own merits to determine whether the employer (and his or her counsel) believes the changes rise to the level of substantial or material.

## H-1B Visa—Corporate Reorganizations

In the late 1990s, amended H-1B petitions were required to be filed if an employer underwent any corporate reorganization. If the employer had a new employer identification number (EIN), then an amended petition was required for its employees. This was called the EIN rule.

### Visa Vocab

An employer identification number (EIN) is basically the equivalent of a corporate social security number.

Frequently when companies were bought and sold, merged, or reorganized, their EIN would change, triggering this filing requirement. A merger of two large public companies, for example, each of which might have hundreds of H-1B employees, often caused the new company to file hundreds of amended petitions.

In many cases the event that caused the EIN to change would have no impact upon the employees. Each employee would have the same job with the same salary at the same location. This was a colossal waste of time and resources for the company as well as for the government. As a result, the rules were changed and the EIN rule was abandoned.

### Visa Vocab

The successor in interest rule specifies that no amended petition is required "where a new corporate entity succeeds to the interests and obligations of the original petitioning employer" provided the terms and conditions of employment do not change.

Now the rules with respect to corporate mergers, acquisitions, and reorganizations at least insofar as they affect H-1B visas are extremely liberal. Based on the successor in interest rule, amended H-1B petitions are almost never required as a result of corporate reorganizations or changes of ownership.

How does one comply with the successor in interest rule? Usually the new employer signs an attestation that it is the successor in interest to the previous employer and places this in the employee's file. Sometimes language to this effect can be put in the transaction documents as well. The reality is that the government no longer has much interest in the impact of corporate transactions on H-1B status, and therefore the issue is moot.

## *L-1 Visas—Changes in Qualifying Relationships*

Corporate mergers, acquisitions, or consolidations that have no impact on H-1B visas (due to the successor in interest rule) can have a profound impact on L-1 (intracompany transferee) visa holders.

The underlying basis for an L-1 visa is a corporate relationship between the overseas company and the U.S. employer. There is no such requirement for the H-1B visa. In fact, the U.S. employer does not need to have any overseas offices at all for an H-1B.

The L-1 visa requires that a qualifying relationship, such as parent-subsidiary, affiliate, or joint venture of branch office, exists between the United States and foreign companies. Changes to this approved ownership structure might have a profound impact on an L visa holder, and therefore require the filing of an amendment of status petition.

The regulations provide that an amended L-1 petition is required when there is:

> ➤ a significant change in the employee's duties (a change from a specialized knowledge position to that of a manager or executive, for example);

> ➤ a transfer from one company in the group structure to another;

> ➤ a change in the qualifying relationship between the companies.

### **Advice of Counsel**

The most common reason that an amendment of status is required of L-1A (multinational executive) employers is that the qualifying relationship between the U.S. employer and the overseas company is affected by some corporate transaction. For example, the parent company sells the assets of the subsidiary for whom the foreign national works.

The most obvious example of when an amendment of status is required is when the link between the foreign and the U.S. company is broken, such as when the overseas parent corporation simply sells all its U.S. assets. Should this happen, there would no longer be a qualifying relationship, and L-1 status would be lost.

The rules become somewhat more complicated in large international organizations that might have dozens of companies in dozens of countries. In those cases, the employer might be able to prove a different qualifying relationship that could keep the L-1 status alive, although per the regulations an amendment of status would still be required.

For our purposes, in corporate transactions where the overseas-U.S. corporate relationship might be severed or changed in any significant way, it is imperative to figure out and assess what impact this might have on you as an L visa holder.

## E-1 and E-2 Visas—Changes in Ownership

As discussed in more detail in chapter 10, the fundamental requirement for the E (investor) visa is that the employer be 50 percent or more owned by a foreign owner—whether an individual or a company. Any corporate change that would impact this will impact E status.

By way of example, if a U.S. company that was wholly owned by a Japanese national were to be sold to a British national, Japanese E visa holders would lose their status. And in this case, an amendment of status would not help them.

In addition, the regulations provide that an amended petition be filed when there is a substantive change in the employer, such as a merger, acquisition, or sale of the employing entity.

### Advice of Counsel

In the case of E employers, the most common cause of an amended petition is that the majority ownership of the U.S. company has changed or disappeared. In cases where the U.S. company is no longer foreign owned, E eligibility may have disappeared entirely so there may be no petition to amend. In these cases, critical foreign workers might change to another NIV status such as L-1 or H-1B, if possible.

A change is considered nonsubstantive for E purposes, however, when such activities would not affect eligibility for E classification. For example, a change in the company's name, the replacement of one foreign owner by another (provided they have the same nationality), or other instances that do not affect the individual's job do not require an amended petition.

With respect to E visas, a good rule of thumb is that any change in the ownership—specifically a change in the percentage owned by the foreign owner—generally requires an amendment of status.

Due to the vagaries of the E visa, even in cases where an amended petition might be required it would be appropriate (or even sometimes required) to send an explanatory letter to the embassy that issued the E visa rather than, or in addition to, filing a petition with USCIS. After all, the E visa falls within the purview of DOS as much as or more than it does USCIS. These cases can become tricky and may require counsel to assess what is required.

In addition to the H-1B, L-1, and E visas, other nonimmigrant categories may have specific rules as to when changes in circumstances require an amendment of status petition to be filed. Often, especially with corporate reorganizations or sales of a company, these are sufficiently sensitive or complicated to require counsel to assist and assess what may be required.

As a general rule, if the reason that you got the visa in the first place—your job, your employer—changes in a way that is materially different, you may need to look into whether an amendment is required.

The eligibility requirements for amending status are the same as for changing status discussed in the preceding chapter, so we don't need to discuss them in more detail here. As a summary, they are:

➤ You were lawfully admitted into the United States as a nonimmigrant

➤ You are in status (and you filed while in status)

➤ You have not committed any act that makes you ineligible to receive an immigration benefit (the government likes you test)

 # Extending Your Status

## In This Chapter

➤ How to extend status

➤ Permitted durations

➤ Are extensions of status generally granted?

In the last two chapters we addressed two critical and complex areas—how to change your status and how to amend your status. We learned that in both cases the single biggest criteria for success was being in status when you ask the government for permission to change or amend your status. Immigration lawyers look at it this way: if you are in status, most problems you may have are fixable; status can be changed, amended, or extended, and petitions can be filed to remedy or delay negative action on your case.

### Visa Vocab

As a reminder, a change of status means your status changes from one alphabetical category to another, such as from B-1 to H-1B. An amendment of status means your status is changed to reflect changes in your employer or your personal situation within the same alphabetical category, such as from H-1B (for employer A) to H-1B (to employer B).

If you are out of status, you are out of luck—at least as far as filing petitions with USCIS goes. Absent extraordinary circumstances, USCIS will simply refuse to consider your case. You may be able to remedy your situation by leaving and reentering the United States with

**Advice of Counsel**

The importance of maintaining status is critical to changing, amending, or extending status.

a visa and therefore acquiring new status (provided you have not been out of status for six months or more), but as a general rule, you will not be able to file a petition with USCIS to do so.

A different situation occurs when you merely want more time in exactly the same status you are in. This is called an extension of status.

# When Can You Extend Status?

Suppose you were issued an L-1 visa, and the visa is valid for three years. When you enter the United States, the immigration inspector admits you for only two years. In this case, there is a disconnect between the validity period of your visa (three years) and your status (two years). When your status (as shown on your I-94 card) is set to expire, you have two ways to extend your status.

One way is to leave the United States and reenter using your still valid L-1 visa. The immigration inspector would then give you a new period of status, probably one more year. You can extend your status each time you reenter the United States if you frequently travel in and out of the country, given that every time you reenter the United States you are given a new I-94 card with a new period of status.

In general, the validity period of the visa is usually the same as the validity period of the status you are granted. In other words, when your status is set to expire, you may also need a new visa stamp—and to get one you may need a new petition approved.

**Advice of Counsel**

An extension of status means your permitted time in the United States is extended. This can be done either by leaving the United States and reentering with a valid visa (assuming you still have a valid visa) or by filing a petition with USCIS requesting that it extend your status. If the petition is approved, USCIS will issue you a new I-94 card with additional time in status, but it will not issue a new visa.

This brings us to the second way to extend your status—filing a petition with USCIS requesting that it extend your status. The process and paperwork to file an extension of status is basically the same as that of a petition to amend or extend status.

Similarly, the basic requirements for extending status are the same as changing or amending status:

➤ You were lawfully admitted into the United States as a nonimmigrant

➤ You are in status (and you file while in status)

➤ You have not committed any act that makes you ineligible to receive an immigration benefit (the government likes you test)

# How Long Can Status Be Extended?

You are permitted to request an extension of status up to the maximum allowable time in your particular visa category. Each category is different.

For example, the (total) maximum allowable time to be in status with an L-1B is five years in two increments—three years plus two years. The first time USCIS approves a visa petition for an L-1B it generally grants the maximum allowable time—in this case, three years. Similarly, the L-1B visa issued by the DOS is valid for three years. Finally, when entering the United States, the immigration inspector generally gives you three years of status on your I-94 card. All your dates line up. This is not always true, but it's easier to follow, so stay with me.

At the end of your initial three-year period with your L-1B visa, you are eligible to request that USCIS grant you another two years of L-1B status to give you a total of five years, the most you can have with an L-1B visa.

You make your request by filing an extension of status petition on your behalf and on the behalf of any family members prior to the expiration of your current L-1B status, before your I-94 card expires. If the extension petition is approved, you (and any family members) will receive an I-797 approval notice. At the bottom of this form will be new I-94 cards for you and each family member (one form for each) with a new two-year period of status. If you are not traveling out of the country during the next two years, this is all you need. You are legally in the United States in valid L-1B status. The government has extended your status.

If you do need to travel abroad, this I-797 approval notice is the basis to obtain a new two-year L-1B visa stamp in your passport just as the initial issuance was the basis for the initial three-year visa.

## Example Please

To request an extension of status, you file an I-129 form with USCIS. In part 2, question 2 of the form, you would tick box B, Continuation of previously approved employment without change with the same employer. As you can see in question 4 directly below that, you are asking the government to "extend the stay of each beneficiary" in the same status that you are currently in when you file.

**Part 2. Information About This Petition** *(See instructions for fee information.)*

1. **Requested Nonimmigrant Classification** *(Write classification symbol)*:

2. **Basis for Classification** *(Check one)*:

   ☐  a. New employment.

   ☑  b. Continuation of previously approved employment without change with the same employer.

   ☐  c. Change in previously approved employment.

   ☐  d. New concurrent employment.

   ☐  e. Change of employer.

   ☐  f. Amended petition.

3. Provide the most recent petition/application receipt number for the beneficiary. If none exists, indicate "N/A."

4. **Requested Action** *(Check one)*:

   ☐  a. Notify the office in **Part 4** so each beneficiary can obtain a visa or be admitted. (**NOTE:** *A petition is not required for an E-1, E-2, H-1B1 Chile/Singapore, or TN visa.*)

   ☐  b. Change each beneficiary's status and extend their stay since he, she, or they are all now in the U.S. in another status *(see instructions for limitations)*. This is available only where you check "New Employment" in **Item 2**, above.

   ☑  c. Extend the stay of each beneficiary since he, she, or they now hold this status.

   ☐  d. Amend the stay of each beneficiary since he, she, or they now hold this status.

   ☐  e. Extend the status of a nonimmigrant classification based on a Free Trade Agreement. *(See Free Trade Supplement for TN and H1B1 to Form I-129.)*

   ☐  f. Change status to a nonimmigrant classification based on a Free Trade Agreement. *(See Free Trade Supplement for TN and H1B1 to Form I-129.)*

5. **Total number of workers in petition** *(See instructions relating to when more than one worker can be included.)*:

Form I-129 (Rev. 01/19/11)Y Page 2

Once the total of five years (three plus two) on your L-1B visa has elapsed, no further extensions are permitted. You may attempt to change your status to another category, of course, assuming you are eligible. Or you may be somewhere in the green card process, which might give you other options. Otherwise, however, you will have to leave the United States.

The maximum permitted time in the United States varies depending on which nonimmigrant visa you have. The time frames for the most common nonimmigrant visas are as follows:

| Nonimmigrant Visa Type | Maximum Total Validity | Permitted Increments |
|---|---|---|
| B-1, B-2 | No limit (in theory) | 6 months at a time |
| H-1B | 6 years (unless PERM was filed at least a year prior to max out date, then indefinite) | 3 years + 2 years + 1 year (1-year extensions thereafter while PERM is in process, 3-year increments once I-140 is approved) |
| L-1A | 7 years | 3 years + 2 years + 2 years |
| L-1B | 5 years | 3 years + 2 years |
| E-1, E-2 | No limit | 2 years |
| O, P | No limit (in theory) | Maximum 2 years at a time— itinerary required to cover requested period for artists, athletes, and other performers |
| TN | No limit | 3 years at a time |

As the above chart should make clear, the E (investor) and TN (NAFTA professional) visas are unusual (and valuable) because there is no maximum period. You can, assuming you remain eligible, hold an E or TN visa forever—which makes them essentially the equivalent (at least in terms of duration) of having permanent residency (a green card).

E and TN visas are procedurally more of a headache than having a green card in one sense: you must continually act to renew the underlying status and visa. A green card once received can be held forever and does not need to be renewed.

**Visa Vocab**

PERM refers to a process for obtaining a green card and the I-140 refers to a different stage of a green card application.

On the other hand, having a visa that you can keep indefinitely is in some ways better than having a green card. As a permanent resident you are deemed a U.S. resident for federal tax purposes and are required to file U.S. tax returns. This is not necessarily true of nonimmigrant visa holders, whose U.S. tax status is determined by how much time they are physically present in the United States.

Finally, the chart above indicates that there is no maximum validity period to a B-1 or B-2 visa. In theory, it can be held forever. The "in theory" qualification is quite important however.

As discussed in chapter 7, the B visa requires the applicant to demonstrate that he or she does not have any intention to reside permanently in the United States. The longer a person is in the United States, the harder this may be to prove. So B cases are heavily scrutinized. USCIS in particular is unlikely to grant ongoing B extensions for business or tourism unless the circumstances are compelling. B extensions for preferential categories such as domestic servants or partners of NIV holders don't face this same challenge. So while you can keep a B visa forever in theory, the government is highly unlikely to let you do so in most circumstances.

## Who Cannot Extend Status

Extending status is permitted for most of the common employment-based NIV as well as the B visa categories, but the following nonimmigrant visa categories are not eligible for status extensions:

> ➤ VW (Visa waiver visitors)

> ➤ C (aliens in transit)

> ➤ D (crewmen)

> ➤ K-1 or K-2 (fiancé(e) or dependent of fiancé(e))

> ➤ S (witness or informant)

> ➤ TWOV (transit without visa)

# Status Extension Problems

For most employment-based nonimmigrant categories, such as H-1B, L-1, or O-1, an extension of status is usually a formality if you are eligible for more time in that category. After all, the underlying substantive basis for the case has already been approved. Unless the job changes or there are other unusual circumstances, the extension is generally approved. But this is not always the case.

## *Exceptions*

One exception is with new office L-1A (multinational executive) petitions. When requesting an extension of status after the first one-year period is up, USCIS looks closely at the nature and size of the business to determine whether its financial strength warrants an extension of the L-1A visa. This new office situation only occurs with the L-1A visa.

B visa extensions also are not automatic. A B-1 or B-2 extension can be looked at almost as if each case is being filed and judged on a stand-alone basis, and for this reason should never be taken for granted.

## **Visa Vocab**

U.S. offices of foreign corporations that have been in existence for less than one year are called new offices.

## *When Extensions Go Wrong*

If your application for an extension of status is denied after your previously approved status has expired and you are still in the United States, you are considered to be out of status. You must cease employment (if such employment was authorized) and leave the United States immediately. In addition, any nonimmigrant visa in your passport that was granted in connection with your classification becomes void. Once your visa is void, you must submit any new visa applications at a U.S. consulate in your home country, not in a third country except in rare cases.

All in all, applications to extend one's status in most employment-based NIV categories should be noncontroversial and processed in the ordinary course, assuming that the applicant is entitled to additional time in the NIV category and is otherwise in status when he or she applies.

If the principal beneficiary's case is approved, the extension of status for spouse and children are almost always approved as well. In certain cases the government might make an error—or the applicants might do so—but it is fair to say that if the beneficiary's case is approved, the dependents' cases will be as well.

## CHAPTER 21

# Visas for Spouses, Children, and Cohabiting Partners

---

### In This Chapter

➤ Dependent visas

➤ Who qualifies

➤ The dependent spouse categories

➤ Cohabiting partners

---

One of the major issues facing foreign nationals in deciding whether or not to come to the United States on a temporary basis with a nonimmigrant visa is whether their spouse, children, or cohabiting partner can get a visa to come as well.

## Dependents

In most cases if the principal applicant is eligible to obtain a nonimmigrant visa, the spouse and children are eligible as well unless something specific to their personal situation makes them ineligible, such as a criminal conviction. Rarely are there any substantive issues in obtaining a visa for the spouse or children of an NIV recipient.

### Visa Vocab

Spouses and children of the principal visa holder are called dependents because their applications are dependent upon the principal's application.

Cohabiting partners who are not married to a nonimmigrant visa holder are not eligible for traditional dependent visa status, as discussed below, but they may apply for B-2 visitor classification to accompany their partner to the United States.

## The Process in Brief

The process for obtaining an NIV is simpler for spouses and children than for the original applicant. Take a customary employment visa, such as the L-1A (multinational executive). The petitioner (in the case of an L-1A, the U.S. employer) applies for an approved petition from USCIS on behalf of the foreign national. At this stage, USCIS does not care (or ask) whether the foreign national has any dependents who will also need visas.

### Advice of Counsel

Most dependents share the same alphabetical category as the principal but have a different number associated with their visas. For example, the dependents of an L-1A visa holder will have L-2 visas, and dependents of an H-1B visa holder will have H-4 visas.

Once USCIS grants the petition, the principal and all dependents apply together for their visas at a consulate. Assuming they present the correct paperwork, pay the correct fees, and do not have any issues in their background that would otherwise make them ineligible to receive a visa, approval of their visas is pretty much a given. Dependents are almost always given a visa with the same expiration date as the principal applicant.

When the time comes for the principal to extend status, which is usually done by filing an extension request with USCIS, the dependents must each separately request an extension of status as well.

### Advice of Counsel

Although there are generally no substantive issues in obtaining dependent visas, each dependent must obtain his or her own visa and is responsible for maintaining his or her own status. A dependent can fall out of status even if the principal applicant is in status, and vice versa.

## Status is Person Specific

Dependents must separately apply for and maintain their own status either through filing petitions with USCIS or by reentering the United States with visas. In this regard their cases are not dependent on the principal applicant—their status is unique to them. For example, if the principal applicant files (and receives) an L-1A extension, he or she will be in status—but that won't help the spouse and kids. Each of them must apply individually, although generally spouses and children all file using the same I-539 form.

When the time comes to obtain new visa stamps, applicants (the principal and each dependent) must apply just as they did when they first obtained their initial visa stamps.

B visas are different because there are no dependent B visas—every applicant must qualify independently.

# Who Qualifies as a Dependent

Obtaining a dependent visa is not rocket science, presuming the individuals qualify as dependents in the first place. There are two kinds of dependents: spouses and children under the age of twenty-one.

The rules are simple and clear, if not very flexible.

## Spouses and Children

A spouse is a dependent if legally married in a heterosexual marriage to the principal. Common law marriages, civil partnerships, girlfriends or boyfriends—in short, any relationship other than a legally recognized civil marriage—do not qualify. Homosexual marriages, even if they are legal in the foreign country, also do not qualify. Nor for that matter, do transsexual marriages, and, yes, since we brought it up there is a specific legal ruling on this very point.

The second type of dependent visa is for children. Children are considered dependents if the parents are the legal parents or guardians and the kids are under twenty-one years of age.

So what happens in situations where someone may have a long-term partner, even one of the same sex, or a common law marriage?

### Visa Vocab

For U.S. federal visa purposes, marriage is solely between a man and a woman. No matter what your personal or political views are, that's the rule in the visa world and there are no exceptions.

## *Cohabiting or Domestic Partners*

The embassy usually issues a B-2 visitor visa for an unmarried partner to accompany a principal applicant. The same holds true for other family members who may not qualify as dependents, such as aunts and uncles or grandparents.

The application process for cohabiting partners is largely the same as with any B visa. In addition to the normal filing requirements, however, the consular officer wants to see evidence of the nature of the relationship between the principal and the B-2 partner, such as:

> ➤ Evidence of a shared residence such as a mortgage statement or a rental agreement

> ➤ A personal statement signed by principal and partner detailing the relationship

> ➤ Statements for joint accounts and assets

> ➤ Photos, testimonials, or similar evidence

In addition, the consul also wants to see that the B-2 partner will be financially supported during the visit to the United States. For this reason, it is advisable for the principal to provide copies of bank statements or evidence of intended employment in the United States.

The B-2 is a tourist visa after all, so the partner is required to overcome the presumption that he or she is intending to immigrate to the United States.

### Advice of Counsel

Once the visa is issued, the beneficiary may apply for admission to the United States as a tourist and is usually given six months of stay to remain in the United States.

The principal who plans to stay in the United States for more than six months should ask the Customs and Border Protection (CBP) officer for a one-year stay at the time of entry to the United States. If the officer does not grant this stay, the partner may apply through USCIS for extensions of stay in increments of up to six months for the duration of the principal's nonimmigrant status in the United States.

Although issuing B-2 visas for partners is common, this solution is less ideal than having a true dependent spouse visa (such as an L-2) for a few reasons.

Cohabiting, or domestic, partners with B-2 visas are required to constantly travel in and out of the States to renew their status or to file extension of status applications every six months. This can be a hassle and expensive.

A second and potentially worse problem sometimes arises upon entry to the United States. Although it is perfectly legal for the domestic partner to have a B visa in these circumstances, sometimes immigration officials do not know this. After all, these are visa rules (DOS), not immigration rules (USCIS). All the immigration inspector sees is a B visitor repeatedly coming and going into the United States or living in the United States on essentially a full-time basis—which is, of course, a no-no. Having to explain the law to a CBP inspector is not a situation you want to be in—even if you are in the right.

In these cases, when domestic partners travel, they often carry a letter from their lawyer explaining the nature and basis of the B visa, and why it is appropriate.

# Dependent Visa Categories

The type of dependent visa is the same whether issued for a spouse or a child. For example, both spouse and child would receive an H-4 visa if the principal was in H-1B status.

The Q (cultural exchange) visa is one of the rare nonimmigrant visa categories with no dependent visa. Technically, the B visa does not offer a dependent visa either. Instead, each dependent applies for a B visa with both principals and dependents following the same rules.

The chart below sets out the various types of dependent visa categories and whether a category allows a spouse to apply and obtain permission to work. We will deal with that topic in the next chapter.

|  | Description |  | Is Spouse Allowed to Work? |
| --- | --- | --- | --- |
| E-1 | Treaty traders and qualified employees | E-1 | Yes |
| E-2 | Treaty investors and qualified employees | E-2 | Yes |
| E-3 | Certain specialty occupation professionals from Australia | E-3 | Yes |
| H-1B | Workers in a specialty occupation, and the following subclassifications: H-1B1—Free Trade Agreement workers in a specialty occupation from Chile and Singapore; H-1B2—specialty occupations related to DOD Cooperative Research and Development projects or coproduction projects; H-1B3—fashion models of distinguished merit and ability | H-4 | No |
| H-2A | Temporary or seasonal agricultural workers | H-4 | No |
| H-2B | Temporary nonagricultural workers | H-4 | No |
| H-3 | Trainees other than medical or academic but including practical trainees in the education of handicapped children | H-4 | No |

| | Description | | Is Spouse Allowed to Work? |
|---|---|---|---|
| I | Representatives of foreign press, radio, film, or other foreign information media | I | No |
| L-1A | Intracompany transferees in managerial or executive positions | L-2 | Yes |
| L-1B | Intracompany transferees in positions utilizing specialized knowledge | L-2 | Yes |
| O-1 | Persons with extraordinary ability in sciences, arts, education, business, or athletics and in motion picture or TV production | O-3 | No |
| O-2 | Persons accompanying solely to assist an O-1 nonimmigrant | O-3 | No |
| P-1A | Internationally recognized athletes | P-4 | No |
| P-1B | Internationally recognized entertainers or members of internationally recognized entertainment groups | P-4 | No |
| P-2 | Individual performer or part of a group entering the United States to perform under a reciprocal exchange program | P-4 | No |
| P-3 | Artists or entertainers, either an individual or group who perform, teach, or coach under a program that is culturally unique | P-4 | No |
| Q-1 | Persons participating in an international cultural exchange program for the purpose of providing practical training and employment, and to share the history, culture, and traditions of the foreign national's home country | N/A | N/A |
| R-1 | Religious workers | R-2 | No |
| TN | North American Free Trade Agreement (NAFTA) temporary professionals from Mexico and Canada | TD | No |

# CHAPTER 22

# Employment Authorization for Spouses of Certain Visa Holders

## In This Chapter

➤ Who qualifies for work permission

➤ The EAD card

➤ How to get one

As we discussed in the previous chapter, in almost all real-world circumstances there is a dependent NIV option for legally married spouses of nonimmigrant visa holders and their children under twenty-one.

A different but related question that is often raised is whether spouses can legally work in the United States. After all, many spouses of foreign NIV holders may also have professions in their home countries. What are their options?

## Who Qualifies

The government has recognized this issue and somewhat begrudgingly has granted a concession to the spouses of certain NIV holders in a limited fashion.

I say *begrudgingly* because this was not always the case. Historically, dependent spouses had no right to work, unless of course they separately and independently qualified for an employment-based work visa. The rules were changed in 2002 to permit certain dependent spouses to obtain work permission.

*Certain* is also a key word, because the rules only permit spouses of particular NIV holders to obtain work permission. Specifically, only spouses holding L (intracompany transferee) or E (investor) dependent visas are eligible to obtain work permission—meaning that spouses of H-1B, O-1, B-1, or other NIVs are out of luck.

In addition, only spouses are eligible—not children, domestic or common law partners, or anyone else.

# The Employment Authorization Document

E and L spouses are not permitted to work simply by virtue of their visa status, however. Rather, these individuals may apply for work permission from USCIS in the form of an employment authorization document (EAD) card.

An EAD card looks very much like a driver's license, as you can see below.

The EAD card can be used in place of the I-9 employment eligibility verification form as evidence that the individual is eligible to work legally in the United States for the period shown at the bottom of the card.

## Advice of Counsel

The holder of an EAD card may work for any U.S. employer—work permission is not employer specific. Ironically, this actually gives the L or E spouses more flexibility in seeking employment than the principals, who have the underlying work visa. A principal's L-1A or E-2 visa is employer specific and nontransferable.

Because the basis for permission to work is tied to a spouse's dependent status, the EAD card is no longer substantively valid if the principal L or E visa holder loses his or her job or otherwise no longer has valid status. Again, the spouse's work permission is entirely dependent on—and derivative to—the principal NIV holder's status.

# The Application Process

The application process is simple, although it may take some time. No interview is required. The dependent spouse files an application with USCIS using the I-765 form. Along with the filing fee, the applicant must include:

> ➤ Proof of the principal's current status, including the petition approval notice

> ➤ I-94 card proving the status of both the principal and the spouse applicants

> ➤ Evidence of the relationship between the principal and the spouse (a copy of the marriage certificate is usually sufficient)

Once approved, the EAD card is mailed to the applicant and is issued for the period of admission but for no more than two years at a time.

Obtaining work permission for L and E spouses generally does not carry with it many substantive issues. In other words, if you are eligible and apply for an EAD card, you will in almost all circumstances receive one.

### *EAD Card in Hand*

Importantly, applicants must have a physical EAD card in hand before they are eligible to work, and they must continue to have a valid card while they are working. Merely applying for an EAD card does not constitute permission to work.

**Advice of Counsel**

The application processing times for an EAD vary greatly, but waits of up to six months are not unheard of.

By the same token, once an EAD card expires, the applicant is no longer eligible to legally work. Therefore, the applicant must apply to renew his or her EAD card well in advance of its expiration. If you are not in possession of a facially valid EAD card, you are not eligible to work—period.

### Advice of Counsel

An EAD card expiring without the holder (or his or her employer) realizing it—or realizing it too late— is a common problem. Because of the long waiting period for EAD cards, there can be a gap in employment eligibility between the expiration of an EAD card and the time a new EAD card is in hand. There is no easy answer to this problem, although by the same token the government is rarely (if ever) aware of the fact that this gap may exist.

## Timing Issues

The basis for spousal work permission is that the principal (that is the L or E visa holder) has entered the United States with a visa and has obtained status. In other words, you as the spouse are not eligible to apply for an EAD card until your spouse enters the United States with visa in hand.

It may take several months after turning in your application for USCIS to issue your EAD card. This means that spouses are at a timing disadvantage in terms of the principal NIV holder. The spouse will not be able to begin working for many months after arrival in the United States, unlike the principal who can begin work immediately upon entering the United States with the appropriate employment-based NIV.

As a result, spouses accompanying NIV holders to the United States are often better off applying for and obtaining their own NIV through an employer (if possible), rather than waiting for their EAD card to be issued. Otherwise, they must factor this timing into their schedules.

The EAD card has its shortcomings, in particular the lengthy processing time and rigid rules governing its expiration. That being said, it does give a simple and important benefit to L and E spouses—the freedom and flexibility to work in the United States.

# CHAPTER 23

# Overstay Issues and the Three- and Ten-Year Bars

## In This Chapter

➤ Staying after your I-94 card has expired

➤ Mandatory penalties

➤ Some potential exceptions

"I overstayed my visa. Am I in trouble?"

The answer to this question is a question—how long have you overstayed?

The depth of trouble you may be in varies tremendously by the length of time you have been in the United States after your I-94 card's expiration date. But let's start from the beginning.

## Overstaying Your Welcome

As you know by now, you are permitted to remain legally in the United States through the period of time shown on your I-94 card provided you do not otherwise violate the terms of your visa. In this situation you are said to be in status.

If you file an extension of your status prior to the expiration date on your I-94 card, you are permitted to remain legally in the United States for up to 240 days while your case is being decided. The fact that you filed a petition before your I-94 card expired, while you were still in status, allows you to maintain your status while the government reviews your case.

But if you have stayed in the United States past the date set forth on your I-94 card without filing a petition to extend or otherwise change your status, you are unlawfully present in the United States and considered to be an overstay.

## What Happens Now?

If you overstay—even by a day—your allotted time in the United Sates, you trigger certain legal penalties. Your visa is deemed void, and, as we saw earlier, USCIS will not accept a petition to amend, extend, or change your status at this point.

Being in overstay subjects you (at least theoretically) to removal proceedings if you are caught. All in all, your legal options are now rather limited.

### Advice of Counsel

If you came to the United States under the VWP and overstayed, you are now no longer permitted to travel on the VWP, meaning any future trips will require you to obtain a visa.

In the view of the U.S. government, status is like pregnancy—you are either in status or not in status. There is no middle ground. Any time spent past your permitted period of status renders you an overstay. In the view of the authorities, you have one option and one option only—you have to leave the country. You have no legal right to remain in the United States and, absent extraordinary circumstances, virtually no chance to get yourself back in status.

Here are the technical legal answers to questions about what happens if you overstay. How this plays out in reality, however, is a bit more complex and depends in large part upon how long your period of overstay is.

## Will the Government Know?

Suppose your I-94 card expires on January 15 but you have a return flight to your home country on January 17. Assuming you make your flight, you will technically be a two-day overstay. Will the government find out? Will it subject you to all the possible legal penalties described above? Although it is possible, this is very unlikely.

When you leave the United States you surrender your I-94 card to the airline officials. They in turn send these to the government where who knows what happens to them—although we strongly suspect they pile up in a warehouse, abandoned and unread. Generally speaking, a minimum amount of time spent as an overstay is simply not noticed or enforced by the government.

In theory—if it were so inclined—the government could mathematically figure out when you entered and when you left the United States and conclude you overstayed by two days. In certain limited circumstances this might occur, for example if you are applying for a visa abroad and the overstay issue is somehow noticed.

The reality is that the government almost never does this—at least for minimum overstay periods. It would be too difficult. In fact, some people lose their I-94 cards or fail to turn them in when they leave the United States. In these cases there is no realistic way for the government to figure out when those people entered the United States and when they left. Consequently, the penalty for a two-day overstay is usually nothing.

That does not mean overstaying a couple of days is a good idea or that you will always get away with it. But it does mean that minimum overstay periods are often undetected and often unpunished. The consequences get more serious, however, when a two-day overstay stretches into two months or longer.

### Advice of Counsel

Keep in mind that passports have entry and departure stamps. If you have a number of date stamps representing repeated entries and departures—particularly under visa waiver—and the length of stay is widely varied, an immigration inspector might conclude that you have overstayed.

# The Three- and Ten-Year Bars

Overstays that stretch into six months definitely create a problem, and these problem are manifested by mandatory penalties known as the three- and ten-year bars.

Simply put, if you overstay more than six months but less than one year, you will be prohibited—barred —from reentering the United States for a period of three years. If you overstay more than one year, you will be barred from reentering the United States for ten years. These are federal bars, and they are nonnegotiable and basically cannot be waived.

### Visa Vocab

The three- and ten-year bars refer to mandatory bars, or bans, from entering the United States if the overstay was more than six months or more than one year, respectively. Put differently:

> ➤ A six-month overstay results in a three-year bar

> ➤ A one-year overstay results in a ten-year bar

These bars come into effect only if you leave the United States and attempt to reenter. If you stay in the United States—even illegally—you may be subject to other government action such as removal, but the three- and ten-year bars do not apply. They are readmission bars.

The net result of this is that once you have overstayed more than six months, you do not have much incentive to leave if you ever want to return to the United States. You are, after all, an overstay—and whether by one month or one year, you are equally out of status. But if you leave, then you face the realistic chance that your overstay will be discovered and you will not be let back into the United States.

### Advice of Counsel

As you may have concluded, the three- and ten-year bars are one major reason why the U.S. immigration system is so screwed up. These bars basically prevent illegal immigrants from leaving the country once they have overstayed more than six months. After all, who wants to risk not being allowed back in? Better to stay put.

# Some Loopholes

You can fix a lot of problems and issues with a good lawyer, but you can't undo the three- and ten-year bars. There are no exceptions, so the best advice is never to trigger the bars in the first place. If you have overstayed by less than six months, it's best to leave the United States before the three-year bar kicks in. If you find you are subject to a three- or ten-year bar, however, don't plan on leaving the United States unless you are willing to run the risk of being denied reentry.

While there are no exceptions, there are some loopholes that you should be aware of.

## *Based on Timing, Not Conduct*

Unlawful presence is not based on any actions that may have violated your status. For example, coming to the United States under visa waiver and immediately beginning to work illegally affects your status but has nothing to do with unlawful presence. As a nonimmigrant you can be deemed to be unlawfully present only if you overstay the date on your I-94 card. Of course, you may be subject to other penalties as a result of your violation of status.

## Advice of Counsel

Immigration lawyers are constantly asked by friends or acquaintances to look at the case of a nanny, housekeeper, or other individual who has "some immigration problems." More often than not the individual is an overstay, sometimes for many years. These friends are usually surprised that there is no legal route or corrective action that can be taken for these individuals given the three- and ten-year bars—short of marriage to a U.S. citizen.

## *Extensions of Status*

If you file an extension of status petition while in status and it is denied, you begin accruing time for purposes of the three- and ten-year bars from the date of denial, not from the expiration date of your original I-94 card. However, if your extension petition was deemed frivolous in that it had no arguable basis in law or fact, or if you are working illegally, then you begin accruing time from when the original I-94 card expired because you would be considered out of status.

## Advice of Counsel

Suppose you file an extension of status petition before your I-94 card expires. You know that it will take two to four months, maybe more, for your case to be reviewed by USCIS. You also know that you are in legal status because the petition is under review. Can you then continue to file petitions with USCIS before the first petition is reviewed, and thus stack up more time? No. The USCIS will not allow you to file numerous petitions to gain more time in status while the first is pending.

## *The Duration of Status (D/S) Categories*

Finally, certain NIV categories do not give a specific date on the I-94 card. For example, the A (diplomat), F (student), G (international organization), M (vocational student), and J (exchange visitor) visa categories relate to a certain activity rather than a preset activity or time period. In these categories it can be difficult to trigger the unlawful presence clock at all.

Take the F-1 student visa, for example. When you enter the United States with an F-1 visa, the inspector annotates your I-94 card with D/S, which means "duration of status." You won't be given a specific date on your I-94 card. Due to the peculiarities of the F visa, the period of your status (the date that normally would be on your I-94 card) is instead shown on your I-20 form.

You cannot begin accruing time toward the three- and ten-year bars if your I-94 card is annotated D/S—such as with the F visa example above— unless the government specifically rules that you are out of status, either when you submit a petition or in a deportation proceeding.

To keep things simple and aboveboard, manage your status, seek good counsel if you have a problem, and don't get in a situation where you are an overstay. An ounce of prevention is worth several tons of cure.

# CHAPTER 24

# The Interplay Between the Visa and the Green Card

### In This Chapter

- ➤ Immigrant intent summary
- ➤ An overview of the green card process
- ➤ Green cards for the family
- ➤ Green cards for employment
- ➤ Options for dual intent holders
- ➤ A lottery for green cards

As we have seen repeatedly throughout our exploration of the U.S. visa laws, the various NIV categories all have a common characteristic—they are temporary. In fact, this is what makes them nonimmigrant visas—their holders are all nonimmigrants as opposed to those seeking permanent residency within the United States as immigrants.

### Visa Vocab

Permanent residency (PR), lawful permanent residency (LPR), and green card all refer to having legal permission to reside permanently in the United States. Permanent residents have most of the rights of U.S. citizens and, importantly, are eligible to work for any U.S. employer.

But not surprisingly, after residing for several years in the United States many NIV holders conclude that they do want to live in the United States on a longer-term basis either as a green card holder or, down the road, as a U.S. citizen. They may have established professional and personal ties in the United States that they do not want to break, or they may not want to return to their home country, particularly if life there is difficult, poor, or unstable. Like millions of others, they may have concluded that life in the United States represents the best option for them and their family.

So the question of how to transform a temporary NIV into long-term residency in the United States comes up for some NIV holders. The answer depends on the NIV category and how it treats the question of immigrant intent.

# Immigrant Intent Revisited

As a brief refresher, one basic eligibility requirement for most NIV categories is that the applicant does not have immigrant intent, the intention of living permanently in the United States. In visa categories such as B (business/tourist), F (student), and J (exchange visitor), proving that you do not have such intent is fundamental to obtaining the visa. These visa holders are not eligible to maintain their current NIV status and apply for permanent residency. If a visa holder is interested in pursuing permanent residency, a change in status that provides for dual intent may be the way to go. Of course, the visa holder must meet the qualifications and requirements of the new status.

### Example Please

The TN (NAFTA professional) classification does not provide for dual intent, however, the H-1B (professional worker) classification does. A TN-1 worker with a bachelor's degree employed in a professional position for a U.S. company that wants to sponsor him or her for a green card may consider changing status to H-1B because the H-1B has similar requirements and the TN worker most likely will qualify for the H-1B.

In short, if you are in an NIV category that permits dual intent such as L (intracompany transferee), H (professional worker), or—to a degree—E (investor), you may be eligible to apply for permanent residency. If you are in any other NIV category, you probably are not eligible—with the exception of being married to a U.S. citizen, which will be discussed below.

# The Green Card Process Overview

The PR process is extremely complicated, with various processes, regulations, and exceptions that are simply beyond the scope of this book to address. So here is a brief overview of the permanent residency process.

The PR process can be broken down into two general paths:

➤ PR based on a family relationship

➤ PR based on sponsorship by an employer

To be eligible for PR in either category, you must be classified under a specific immigrant visa (IV) preference category and an IV number must be available to you. With one exception, the U.S. government limits the number of IVs available in each preference category each fiscal year. Oftentimes there are more applicants requesting IVs than there are available numbers.

**Visa Vocab**

This backlog of IV numbers is called retrogression. IV availability is tracked by the DOS, and the available numbers are updated on a monthly basis. IV numbers are made public via the DOS's Visa Bulletin, which is posted on the DOS website.

# The Family-Based Green Card

Family-based PR is available for foreign nationals who fall under one of the following preference categories:

➤ Spouses and unmarried children under the age of twenty-one of U.S. citizens

➤ Unmarried sons and daughters of U.S. citizens

➤ Spouses and children, and unmarried sons and daughters of U.S. permanent residents

➤ Married sons and daughters of U.S. citizens

➤ Brothers and sisters of adult U.S. citizens

Spouses and unmarried children under the age of twenty-one of U.S. citizens are given preference above all PR applicants. In fact, they are the only category of PR applicants (family- or employment-based) for whom IV numbers are immediately available. The IV retrogression does not apply to these applicants. So you can see that PR via marriage to a U.S. citizen is the quickest and easiest route to a green card.

### Immediate Relative Petitions

A person with NIV status who lawfully marries a U.S. citizen is eligible to file an I-130 petition for alien relative and an I-485 application to register permanent residence or adjust status. In this situation, absent fraud or other exigent circumstances, any NIV holder physically present in the United States may apply for a green card by virtue of marriage to a U.S. citizen. The intent issue does not apply to these cases, regardless of the applicant's NIV status.

Applicants in the other family-based categories are subject to IV availability. The IV retrogression does not keep an applicant from filing an I-130 petition for an alien relative, but the retrogression could mean the green card won't be issued for several years. IV applicants who are in the United States in another NIV status are required to maintain or extend that status to remain in the United States legally while waiting for an IV number to become available.

# The Employment-Based Green Card

The PR process based upon employment varies widely depending upon the type of position being offered and the applicant's educational and work experience. The options for employment-based PR are:

> ➤ Being offered permanent employment by a U.S. employer that sponsors you

> ➤ Being an investor or entrepreneur who is making an investment in an enterprise that creates new U.S. jobs

> ➤ Being eligible to self-petition (sponsor yourself) as an alien of extraordinary ability in your field or being granted a national interest waiver

> ➤ Being considered a special immigrant such as one with NATO-6 nonimmigrant status or a physician national interest waiver in a job such as that of broadcaster, international organization employee, or religious worker that allows you to apply directly for a green card.

## Preference Categories

As with family-based applicants, employment-based PR applicants are placed in preference categories depending upon the type of position they are being offered and their credentials. The employment-based preference categories are:

**Visa Vocab**

A national interest waiver is for PR applicants seeking a waiver of the labor certification requirement because their work is of great benefit to the U.S. national interest.

> ➤ First preference: Multinational managers and executives, aliens of extraordinary ability, and outstanding researchers and professors

> ➤ Second preference: Those with advanced degrees or exceptional ability, and those with national interest waivers

> ➤ Third preference: Skilled workers, professionals, and other workers

> ➤ Fourth preference: Certain special immigrants such as returning residents, people reacquiring U.S. citizenship, and religious workers

> ➤ Fifth preference: Employment creators (investors and entrepreneurs)

The most common preference categories used by NIV holders are the first, second, and third preference categories, so we will focus on these categories for now.

Generally, first preference category workers are considered priority workers and IV numbers in this category are typically current and available. Therefore, workers in this category usually do not have to worry about being subject to the IV retrogression.

If a priority worker qualifies as a multinational manager or executive, an alien of extraordinary ability, or an outstanding researcher, the PR process is relatively straightforward. The petitioning U.S. employer may file an I-140 immigrant worker petition with USCIS confirming the offer of permanent employment, and if the employer wishes to apply for adjustment of status, it may do so concurrently with the I-140.

Workers applying as aliens of extraordinary ability or for a national interest waiver in the second preference category are eligible to self-petition; they are not required to have a U.S. employer sponsor their I-140.

For all other second and third preference category workers, the PR process takes three steps.

The first step is called labor certification, or PERM. The petitioning U.S. employer must test the U.S. labor market by performing a number of recruitment efforts to ensure there are no qualified U.S. citizens or permanent residents available for the position. If there is even one qualified and available U.S. citizen or permanent resident who is qualified and interested in the position, the labor certification cannot be filed with the Department of Labor (DOL) and the PR process cannot proceed.

**Visa Vocab**

PERM stands for the Program Electronic Review Management system. This system was introduced in 2005 to process labor certification applications.

If there are no qualified or available U.S. citizens or permanent resident workers available, the labor certification can be filed with the DOL. The date the labor certification is filed is called the priority date, which will be relevant later in the process.

The second step in the process is to file the I-140 immigrant worker petition with USCIS. Dependent family members (spouses and children under the age of twenty-one) who intend to immigrate with the beneficiary can be included on the I-140 petition.

The final step in the employment-based PR process is changing status to permanent resident. The timing for this filing depends upon the IV availability in the beneficiary's preference category. The beneficiary's case is placed in a queue according to priority date with all the other applicants in that preference category.

If there is IV availability in the category, the beneficiary's priority date is considered current and the final step of the process can be filed. If IVs are not available and the preference category is retrogressed, the beneficiary must wait until the priority date is current to file the change in status to permanent resident.

Once the priority date is current, the applicant can proceed via one of two methods:

➤ Filing the I-485 adjustment of status: The I-485 requires that all applicants (the beneficiary and any dependent family members applying with him or her) have maintained legal status while in the United States. An applicant who has had a lapse in nonimmigrant visa status while in the United States might not qualify for this process.

The beneficiary and dependent family members must be physically present in the United States when the I-485 documentation is filed with USCIS. Each applicant (beneficiary, spouse, and each dependent child) must submit an individual I-485 and each may apply for work authorization (EAD) and travel authorization (advance parole). USCIS approves most employment-based I-485 applications without requiring an interview, and the green cards are mailed to the applicant(s). Should an interview be required, USCIS will schedule that appointment with the local office closest to the applicant's home address.

➤ Applying via IV consular processing: The applicant completes the final step of the PR process outside of the United States. After the I-140 is approved by USCIS, the case is sent to the DOS for final processing through the U.S. consulate in the beneficiary's home country. The applicant and any family members are required to attend an interview at the U.S. consulate. If approved, the consulate issues an immigrant visa in each applicant's passport to allow entry to the United States as a permanent resident. The actual green card is then mailed to the applicant's address in the United States.

# Permanent Residency Options for NIV Holders

The PR options for NIV holders typically vary depending upon their current NIV status.

## *L-1A Managers and Executives*

If you qualified for the L-1A manager or executive intracompany transferee visa category and now your U.S. employer wants to sponsor you for PR, it is likely that you will qualify in the first preference category as a multinational manager or executive. Specifically, you will need to prove that you worked for the company abroad for at least one year within the past three years in a managerial or executive capacity.

### Advice of Counsel

While the criteria to qualify for an L-1A intracompany transferee visa requires the U.S. position to be managerial or executive in nature, the applicant's experience with the company abroad does not have to be of a managerial or executive nature. However, to be classified as a multinational manager or executive for PR purposes, the applicant must show that prior experience with the company (at least one year in the past three years) was in a managerial or executive capacity.

Additionally, the sponsoring U.S. company must prove that it maintains the qualifying relationship (as explained in chapter 9) with the beneficiary's prior employer abroad.

## *L-1B Specialized Knowledge Employees and H-1B Professional Workers*

If you are currently in H-1B or L-1B status, the U.S. position you hold is highly specialized and your qualifications for that position probably include a university degree and/or extensive professional experience in the specialty field. As such, your position and experience should qualify you in either the second or third preference category.

To qualify for the second preference category—members of professions holding advanced degrees—you must hold an advanced degree (such as a master's degree or PhD). In addition, the position with the company must fall under a job classification that is deemed by DOL to require a master's degree or higher. The job classification is determined in the labor certification process.

Most second and third preference applicants are subject to the IV retrogression, which can mean a very long wait for the PR process to be completed. Applicants in H-1B status who face long-pending PR processes have the option to extend their H-1B status beyond the six-year maximum provided the PERM labor certification was filed with DOL at least one year before the expiration date.

Alternatively, if the PERM was not filed before the start of the sixth year of H-1B status but the I-140 has been approved, the applicant is eligible for extensions of H-1B status in three-year increments. Dependent family members are eligible for extension of H-4 status but not for extension of H-1B status.

### Example Please

A PR applicant and her spouse are both currently in the United States in H-1B status. The PR applicant has an approved PERM as well as an approved I-140 in her name, so when her sixth year of H-1B time expires, she is eligible to apply for a three-year extension. However, her spouse's U.S. employer did not sponsor him for a green card, therefore he does not have a PERM or an I-140 showing him as the primary beneficiary. When his sixth year of H-1B time expires, he is not eligible for an extension of H-1B status based upon his wife's PR process, even though he may be listed on her I-140 petition. He must then change status to H-4 dependent or another NIV status to remain in status.

Unfortunately these provisions apply only to H-1B visa holders. L-1B visa holders, for instance, are not eligible to extend their status upon a pending PR process beyond the five-year maximum.

## O-1 Extraordinary Ability

If you are in O-1 status, you have exhibited to USCIS that you meet the criteria as an individual of extraordinary ability (EA) in your field. Meeting this threshold may also qualify you for PR in the first preference category as an individual of extraordinary ability or possibly as an outstanding professor or researcher (OR).

The EA classification is for individuals who can demonstrate sustained national or international acclaim in the sciences, arts, education, business, or athletics. The regulatory criteria to qualify for PR in the EA category are similar to the regulatory criteria for O-1 status as outlined in chapter 11.

The OR classification is for individuals who are recognized internationally as outstanding in a specific academic field and have three-years' experience in research or teaching in the academic field. The permanent position being offered to the beneficiary must be:

➤ A tenure or tenure track teaching position within an institution of higher education;

➤ A comparable position at an institution of higher education to conduct research;

➤ A comparable position to conduct research at a private company that employs at least three full-time researchers and has accomplished achievements in the applicant's academic field.

For classification as an OR, the beneficiary must prove at least two of the following regulatory criteria:

➤ Receipt of a nationally or internationally recognized prize or award in the applicant's academic or research field

➤ Membership in associations in the applicant's academic or research field of expertise that requires outstanding achievements of its members

➤ Published material in professional publications written by others about the applicant's work in the academic or research field

➤ Participation on a panel or individually as a judge of the work of others in the academic or research field

➤ Original scientific or scholarly research contributions to the academic or research field

➤ Authorship of scholarly books or articles in the applicant's academic or research field that appear in scholarly journals with international circulation

As with the O-1 visa, simply submitting enough evidence to cover the required criteria does not ensure a successful EA or OR petition. The preponderance of evidence must also show the beneficiary has sustained national or international acclaim in his or her particular field (for the EA petition) or is recognized internationally as outstanding in a specific academic field (for the OR petition).

# The Green Card Lottery

As strange as it may sound, you heard correctly. It is called the Diversity Visa (DV) Lottery Program and applicants from all over the world (whether they are currently in the United States or not) are eligible to apply.

The DV lottery is run annually by the DOS, which issues 50,000 visa numbers and randomly selects individuals through a computer-generated lottery. The selected applicants are then eligible to apply for a green card.

As the name indicates, the purpose of the lottery is diversity; therefore the number of immigrants coming to the United States from specific areas of the world is taken into consideration for the lottery process. A greater number of DVs are provided to global regions with lower rates of immigration to the United States, and no DVs are provided for nationals of countries sending more than 50,000 immigrants to the United States within the past five years.

The process for the lottery begins at the start of each new fiscal year (which is October 1 for the DOS). There is an official online entry registration period, which typically runs for four to five weeks starting the first week of October. The selection process of the DV lottery is typically completed by May of the year following the registration period. If you are selected by the DV lottery, you are eligible to apply for a green card after the start of DOS's next fiscal year.

### Example Please

Those who apply for the DV lottery in October of 2011 find out in May of 2012 if they were selected. Those who were selected are eligible to apply for a green card no earlier than October 1, 2012.

If you are interested in applying for the DV lottery, you should first consider if you are eligible based on the following factors.

## Your Home Country

You must be a native of a country that is eligible for the DV lottery. A list of DV-eligible countries is posted on the DOS website each year in advance of the open registration period. If your country of birth is not included on the list, you still may be eligible to apply if:

> ➤ Your spouse was born in an eligible country and you plan to enter the United States simultaneously

> ➤ One of your parents was born in an eligible country

## Your Education and Experience

You must also meet either the education or work experience requirement of the DV program. You must have one of the following:

> ➤ A high school education or its foreign academic equivalent, defined as successful completion of a twelve-year course of elementary and secondary education. Only formal courses of study meet this requirement; correspondence programs or equivalency certificates, such as the GED, are not acceptable. Documentary proof of education or work experience must be presented to the consular officer at the time of the visa interview.

> ➤ At least two years of work experience within the past five years in an occupation requiring at least two years of training or experience to perform. The DOL's O*NET OnLine database is used to determine qualifying occupations. To qualify for a DV on the basis of work experience, the applicant's work experience must have been within an occupation that is designated on O*NET as job zone 4 or 5, typically a professional job requiring a minimum of a bachelor's degree.

### Visa Vocab

The Occupational Information Network (O*NET) offers a compilation of occupations and a description of their standard job duties, including the type and amount of experience typically required to perform the duties of each occupation.

All applications must be submitted electronically (there are no paper applications) via the DOS website; you cannot enter the DV lottery through USCIS. The DV entry form (E-DV) is made accessible only during the registration period. There is no charge to enter the DV lottery.

### Advice of Counsel

There have been instances of fraudulent green card lottery websites. If you find a website that requires a charge to complete the DV lottery form, it is not an official site. The U.S. government does not charge to download and complete the E-DV form. The DOS website is the only place where lottery applications can be submitted.

While there are 50,000 IVs available for the DV lottery, they are not all available by the following October 1. The IV numbers are parceled out by the DOS, and DV lottery selectees cannot apply for their green card until their number has been called, similar to immigrant visa retrogression. DOS updates these numbers monthly on its Visa Bulletin, which is posted on its website.

If you are selected in the lottery and have maintained legal status in the United States when your number is called, you may be eligible to apply for adjustment of status. If you are outside of the United States and are selected in the lottery, you would apply for your immigrant visa through the U.S. consulate in your home country.

It is important to note that simply applying for the DV lottery is not an application for a green card. This is an important distinction that can come into play with individuals who have or are applying for an NIV that is not covered by dual intent such as a B (business or tourist), F (student), or M (vocational student) visa. You may enter the DV lottery and still maintain your nonimmigrant intent. However, if you are selected in the DV lottery and you submit your adjustment of status application or apply for your immigrant visa, you are considered an intending immigrant.If you file an extension of your status prior to the expiration date on your I-94 card, you are permitted to remain legally in the United States for up to 240 days while your case is being decided. The fact that you filed a petition before your I-94 card expired, while you were still in status, allows you to maintain your status while the government reviews your case.

But if you have stayed in the United States past the date set forth on your I-94 card without filing a petition to extend or otherwise change your status, you are unlawfully present in the United States and considered to be an overstay.

# CHAPTER 25

# Common Questions and Issues While in the United States

## In This Chapter

➤ Social Security numbers

➤ Driver's license

➤ Paying U.S. taxes

➤ Issues with the I-94 card

➤ Children of nonimmigrants born in the United States

Once you have entered the United States, you'll have to follow laws that have been set forth for all residents, such as obtaining a Social Security number and a driver's license, and paying taxes. You may have questions about your children's citizenship and keeping track of your I-94 card as well.

## What is a Social Security Number?

The Social Security number (SSN) is a nine-digit number issued by the U.S. government. People who work in the United States need to provide an SSN to their employers, who need it to report their wages for tax purposes. You are not required to have an SSN before you begin working, though.

An SSN is also required for certain basic business transactions such as opening a bank account, obtaining a credit card, or completing U.S. tax forms. When you are in the United

States, you are asked for your SSN in all sorts of circumstances, so getting one is pretty important.

### Advice of Counsel

SSNs are issued to U.S. citizens, green card holders, and nonimmigrants who are authorized to work in the United States such as work visa holders or those who have an employment EAD.

You may apply for your SSN once you arrive in the United States pursuant to your work visa or once your work authorization (such as an EAD) has been issued. You are required to appear in person at the local Social Security Administration (SSA) office, where you can complete the required form. You must also provide original evidence of your identity, your work authorized status, and age. Your passport with visa and your original I-94 card usually suffices. Once you apply, you should receive your Social Security card in the mail within a few weeks.

### Advice of Counsel

Wait approximately ten days after arriving in the United States before going to an SSA office to apply for your SSN because it can take several days for the CBP records to appear in the SSA's system. If you appear at an SSA office before its system is updated with your legal work status, you will be turned away and asked to apply for your SSN at a later date.

B visa holders and other individuals who are not authorized to work in the United States are typically not eligible to obtain an SSN, but they are eligible to apply for an individual taxpayer identification number (ITIN). Issued by the U.S. Internal Revenue Service (IRS), an ITIN is a nine-digit tax processing number. Applicants can obtain an ITIN either by applying through the mail or at their local IRS office.

# Obtaining a Driver's License

Each of the fifty U.S. states issues its own driver's licenses and state identification cards, which can be used anywhere in the United States. Different classes of licenses are issued depending on the type of vehicle—car, motorcycle, truck, or commercial—you drive. But before a driver's license or state identification card can be issued to a nonimmigrant, the applicant must show proof of legal immigration status.

When you have a driver's license, there is no need for you to get an identification card. A driver's license is used for identification purposes—even more so than a passport—in most daily transactions such as cashing checks, opening bank accounts, traveling within the United States, and as proof of legal age to buy alcohol and tobacco.

### Visa Vocab

A state driver's license allows you to operate a motor vehicle and doubles as a form of identification. An identification card is used for identification purposes only; it does not authorize you to operate a motor vehicle.

The rules and regulations for obtaining a driver's license varies depending on which state you live in. Most states require that you pass written, road, and vision tests. But some states allow foreign licenses to be used as proof of an individual's ability to operate a motor vehicle, thus not requiring the individual to take a road test.

### Advice of Counsel

Each U.S. state has a Division of Motor Vehicles (DMV) that determines specific requirements for obtaining and renewing a driver's license, but in 2005 the federal government got involved via the REAL ID Act. The federal guidelines implemented by the REAL ID Act set new standards, such as using digital photos and certain security features, for driver's licenses and ID documents issued by each state.

A state-issued driver's license is recognized in all fifty U.S. states, but if you move from one state to another, you are usually required to apply for a license in your new home state. It is advisable to do this as soon as possible after you move. Typically you can transfer your out-of-state license to your new home state. This process differs from state to state, but in general you have to take another vision and/or written test.

# Do I Have to Pay U.S. Taxes?

If you intend to live in the United States on a full-time basis with an NIV, you will most likely have to pay state and federal taxes. Let's leave aside the former because each state has different rules and regulations, although in many cases they track the federal rules. The discussion that follows addresses only U.S. government, or federal, tax rules.

The IRS applies two types of classification to non-U.S. citizens for U.S. federal tax purposes: resident and nonresident aliens.

## *Resident Aliens*

Resident aliens are generally taxed in the same manner as U.S. citizens. This means that their worldwide income is subject to U.S. tax and must be reported on their U.S. tax return. You are considered a resident alien for tax purposes if you are a green card holder or if you meet the substantial presence test for the calendar year.

To meet this test, you must be physically present in the United States for at least 31 days during the current year and 183 days during the three-year period that includes the current year and the two preceding years. To come up with this number, figure in all the days you were present in the United States during the current year, one-third of the days you were present in the United States during the preceding year, and one-sixth of the days you were present in the United States the year before that.

### Example Please

Suppose you were physically present in the United States for 120 days in each of the years 2008, 2009, and 2010. To determine if you meet the substantial presence test for 2010, you would count the full 120 days of presence in 2010, 40 days in 2009 (one-third of 120), and 20 days in 2008 (one-sixth of 120). Since the total for the three-year period is 180 days, you haven't met the 183-day minimum so you are not considered a resident under the substantial presence test for 2010.

There are some exceptions and some complicated formulas that are involved, but in a nutshell the substantial presence test means that if you are physically present in the United States for more than half of each year, you will be subject to U.S. federal taxation. And, of course, if you have a green card, you are subject to federal taxation—full stop.

## Nonresident Aliens

You are considered a nonresident alien if you are not a green card holder and you do not pass the substantial presence test. In other words, even though you have an NIV you may not be subject to U.S. federal taxation.

### Advice of Counsel

Tax issues can be complex and sticky—we strongly suggest you consult with your accountant or tax adviser when planning your NIV tax strategy. The guidance set forth above is just to give you the lay of the land. Consult a professional!

Nonresident aliens are taxed on income from sources within the United States. They must file a U.S. tax return if they are engaged or considered to be engaged in a trade or business in the United States during the year even if the income did not come from a trade or business conducted in the United States, there was no income from U.S. sources, or the income is exempt from income tax.

If you are a nonresident alien student, teacher, or trainee in the United States on an F (student), J (exchange visitor), M (vocational student), or Q (international cultural exchange) visa, you are considered engaged in a trade or business in the United States. You must file a U.S. federal tax return only if you have income that is subject to tax, such as wages, tips, scholarship and fellowship grants, dividends, etc. Finally, please note that F, J, M, and Q visas are exempt from Social Security and Medicare taxes.

### Visa Vocab

Medicare is a U.S. government program that provides health insurance coverage to people over the age of sixty-five, people under the age of sixty-five who have a permanent disability, and those who meet other specific criteria.

### Visa Vocab

Medicaid is a government program designed to help low-income families who are unable to afford medical costs. Eligibility depends on your immigration status and is determined on a state-by-state basis.

The U.S. tax process begins at the start of each calendar year. U.S. employers are required to send a W-2 form to employees, which report the employee's annual wages and the amount of taxes withheld from his or her paycheck from the previous year. Nonemployees such as independent contractors receive a 1099 form reporting their income.

April 15th is commonly known in the United States as Tax Day. Individuals who are employees or self-employed and receive wages or unemployment compensation subject to U.S. income tax withholding are required to file their tax returns by this date. If you cannot file your return by the due date, an extension can be requested from the IRS.

The U.S. tax code can be quite confusing for U.S. citizens let alone someone who is new to the United States. The IRS has many publications on its website devoted to educating nonresidents about their tax liabilities, but it is often advisable for nonresidents to seek professional tax assistance. Foreign students and scholars in the United States can usually seek tax assistance from their sponsoring academic institution or program.

If you are a nonimmigrant visa holder and intend to apply for a green card, you may be required to show if you were required to file income tax returns for the three most recent years preceding your adjustment of status application. Therefore, if you plan to seek permanent residency in the United States, it is important that your U.S. taxes are handled correctly and legally.

### Advice of Counsel

A very simple suggestion: staple your I-94 card onto a blank page of your passport. Also, make a photocopy of it and keep that in a separate place.

# I Lost My I-94 Card

Your I-94 card is a very important document because it proves the validity of your stay in the United States. Unfortunately, it is only a piece of paper and can be easily misplaced, stolen, or mutilated. If this happens, you should apply for a replacement card immediately with an I-102 form, which can be filed with USCIS to request a replacement card.

There is a fee to file the I-102 form, and USCIS can take several months to process it and issue the new I-94 card. However, the filing is critical as it proves that you attempted to correct the situation.

You will receive a receipt shortly after filing, which you should carry with you to prove that you have requested the replacement. Your passport, your U.S. visa stamp in your passport, your driver's license—not one of these documents is proof of your legal status in the United States. Your I-94 card is the only and most important document showing that you are in the United States legally.

You might ask, "What if I'm leaving that United States soon? I really don't have to apply for a replacement because it just gets turned in at the airport anyway."

This is really not advisable and leads us to. . .

# Turning in Your I-94 Card

Each time you leave the United States, you are required to surrender your original I-94 card, except if you are a Canadian citizen and have been issued an I-94 card stamped for multiple entries.

If you forget to surrender your I-94 card or as in the case above you lost it while you were in the United States, never replaced it, and just left the United States, your departure record will not be properly updated with the immigration authorities, which will cause problems.

### Example Please

Let's say you entered the United States as a B-2 tourist for vacation and you were given a ninety-day period of stay. You remained in the United States for only thirty days and left, but you failed to turn in your I-94 card. Because of this, CBP is not aware that you left, your file remains open in the system, and after the ninetieth day passes you are classified as an overstay. Six months later, when you try to reenter the United States for another vacation, CBP checks your record, sees an overstay, and denies you entry and/or cancels your current visa.

Making sure your departure record is updated can be especially beneficial if you have an H-1B (professional worker) or L-1(intracompany transferee) visa, both of which have a maximum period of allowed stay in the United States. Technically, only the days you spend physically in the United States in H-1B or L-1 status count against that maximum allowable period of stay. Any time you spend outside of the United States while your H-1B or L-1 visa is valid is not considered time spent against your allowable period of stay. This time outside of the United States can later be recaptured and added on to the amount of time you can work in the United States. Therefore, an accurate reflection of how much time an H-1B or an L-1 visa holder has physically been in the United States is quite important.

If you have left the United States and are still in possession of the I-94, it is in your best interest to forward it to USCIS so that your record is corrected. You should complete the back of the card listing the port of departure and date of departure from the United States and the carrier/flight information. You should also prepare a letter explaining the error and include proof of your departure, such as a flight itinerary or boarding pass showing your departure details, or entry stamps in your passport indicating you entered another country after you left the United States. If you no longer have the original I-94 card, explain that in your letter as well.

You should not send the I-94 card and documentation to the U.S. consulate in your home country—remember the consulate is run by the DOS, not USCIS. The documentation should be sent to USCIS, specifically: DHS-CBP SBU, 1084 South Laurel Road, London, Kentucky, 40744 USA.

# Children Born in the United States

Under the Fourteenth Amendment of the U.S. Constitution, children born in the United States to foreign citizen parents have claim to U.S. citizenship. If you would like U.S. citizenship for your child, it is not necessary to apply via the naturalization process; you simply apply for a U.S. passport for your child based solely upon his or her birth in the United States. All minors regardless of age must have their own U.S. passport when traveling internationally by air.

Passport issuance is handled through the DOS, and you are required to physically appear at a local passport services office to submit the application.

### Advice of Counsel

Children born in the United States have American nationality. Period.

You are not required to apply for a U.S. passport for your child. If you prefer to apply for a foreign passport under the nationality provisions of your home country, you may do so; however, your child will then require subsequent derivative status to remain in the United States, such as a dependent visa of your current status.

A natural question in this process is: "Can my child have dual citizenship?" In other words, can a child be both a U.S. citizen and a citizen of the parents' home country?

Although the United States and Canada follow the legal principles of *jus soli*, U.S. law recognizes the principles of *jus sanguinis* and allows that a U.S. citizen is not precluded from dual nationality that is obtained through birth in the United States to nationals of another country.

### Visa Vocab

*Jus sanguinis* means a person's citizenship is determined by that of his or her parents' citizenship. *Jus soli* means a person's nationality is determined by the territory within which he or she was born.

A child with dual nationality should use his or her U.S. passport to enter and leave the United States. Also, it is important to keep in mind that although the U.S. government maintains provisions allowing dual nationality, the government of your home country may not.

# Glossary

**amendment of status:** status is changed within the same alphabetical category to reflect changes in your personal situation

**beneficiary:** visa holder

**blanket petition:** an approval notice for a specific company that allows any of its employees to apply at a consulate for an L-1 visa

**biometrics:** fingerprinting

**cap:** the number of new H-1B petitions USCIS is permitted to issue for each federal fiscal year, which begins October 1

**change of status:** status changes from one alphabetical category to another

**class A port of entry:** a port where any foreign national may apply for entry to the United States

**consular officer, or consul:** the issuing official

**consulate:** the section of the embassy that issues visas

**green card:** a card that identifies a foreign national as a permanent resident of the United States

**immigrant:** a resident from another country who either has or is in the process of obtaining lawful permanent residency in the United States

**immigration inspector:** a Customs and Border Protection (CBP) agent at a port of entry

**jus sanguinis:** a rule that a person's citizenship is determined by that of his or her parents' citizenship

**jus soli:** a rule that a person's nationality is determined by the territory within which he or she was born

**kickback:** a notice of intent to deny

**labor certification:** a process of proving that there are no qualified U.S. workers for the position being offered

**nonimmigrant:** someone who is not an immigrant or a U.S. citizen and is not entitled to remain permanently in the United States

**overstay:** staying in the United States past the date set forth on your I-94 card without filing a petition to extend or otherwise change your status

**portability:** the ability of foreigners with H-1B visas to begin working for a new employer with their H-1B visas as soon as they file the petition with USCIS

**retrogression:** The backlog of immigrant visas

**secondary inspection (or secondary):** additional interrogation by an immigration inspector before being allowed into the United States

**status:** the legal situation of a nonimmigrant in the United States (compare to *visa*)

**unlawful presence:** being in the United States past the expiration date on your I-94 card

**Visa Waiver Program:** a program that permits nationals of certain specified countries to travel to the United States without a visa

**visa:** the stamp in your passport (compare to *status*)

# APPENDIX B

# Acronyms

**CBP:** Customs and Border Protection; admits foreign nationals into the United States

**CEO:** Chief Executive Officer

**CFO:** Chief Financial Officer

**COO:** Chief Operating Officer

**CPT:** curricular practical training

**DHS:** Department of Homeland Security

**DMV:** Division of Motor Vehicles

**DOB:** date of birth

**DOL:** Department of Labor

**DOS:** U.S. Department of State; issues visas

**D/S:** duration of status

**DSO:** designated school official

**DV:** diversity visa

**EA:** extraordinary ability

**EAD:** employment authorization document

**ECFMG:** Educational Commission for Foreign Medical Graduates

**E-DV:** DV entry form

**EIN:** employer identification number

**ESTA:** Electronic System for Travel Authorization

**FMG:** foreign medical graduate

**FR:** Federal Register

**ICE:** Immigration and Customs Enforcement

**iCERT:** the electronic system used to file an LCA

**IMBRA:** international marriage broker regulation

**IMG:** international medical graduate

**INS:** Immigration and Naturalization Service

**IRS:** Internal Revenue Service

**IT:** information technology

**ITIN:** individual taxpayer identification number

**IV:** immigrant visa

**LCA:** labor condition application

**LP:** lawfully present

**LPR:** lawful permanent residency

**NAFTA:** North American Free Trade Agreement

**NATO:** North Atlantic Treaty Organization

**NIV:** nonimmigrant visa

**NOID:** notice of intent to deny

**NVC:** National Visa Center

**O*NET:** Occupational Information Network

**OPT:** optional practical training

**OR:** outstanding professor or researcher

**PDSO:** principal designated school official

**PERM:** program electronic review management

**PLC:** public limited company

**PR:** permanent residency

**SEVIS:** student and exchange visitor information system

**SSA:** Social Security Administration

**SSN:** Social Security number

**STEM:** science, technology, engineering, and math

**TSA:** Transportation Security Administration

**USCIS:** United States Citizenship and Immigration Services; approves certain types of visas

**US-VISIT:** United States visitor and immigrant status indicator technology

**VWP:** Visa Waiver Program

# APPENDIX C

# Selected Visas

**A-1:** foreign government officials: ambassadors, public ministers, career diplomats or consular officers, or immediate family

**A-2:** foreign government officials: other foreign government officials or employees, or immediate family

**A-3:** foreign government officials: attendants, servants, or personal employees of A-1 or A-2, or immediate family

**B-1:** business visitor; temporary visa for business travelers and domestic servants

**B-2:** tourist; temporary visitor visa for pleasure or medical treatment

**C:** aliens in transit

**D:** crewmen

**E-1:** treaty trader

**E-2:** treaty investor

**E-3:** Australian specialty occupation professional

**F-1:** academic student

**G:** international organization

**H-1B:** professional worker; professionals who come temporarily to the United States to perform a specialty occupation

**H-1B2:** aliens performing cooperative research and development projects

**H-1B3:** fashion model

**H-2A:** temporary or seasonal agricultural worker

**H-2B:** temporary or seasonal workers other than agricultural

**H-3:** professional trainee

**H-4:** spouses and children under the age of twenty-one of H-1, H-2, and H-3 visa holders

**I:** representative of foreign information media

**I-1:** representatives of foreign media

**J-1:** exchange visitor

**K-1:** fiancé(e) of a U.S. citizen

**K-2:** minor child of fiancé(e) of U.S. citizen

**K-3:** spouse of a U.S. citizen

**K-4:** children of K-3 visa holders

**L-1A:** intracompany transferee (executive, managerial), or multinational executive; executives who are continuing employment with an international firm or corporation

**L-1B:** intracompany transferee (specialized knowledge worker); professionals who are continuing employment with an international firm or corporation

**L-2:** dependents of L-1 visa holders

**M-1:** vocational or other nonacademic student

**NATO-6:** civilian NATO employees and their unmarried sons and daughters

**O-1A:** aliens possessing extraordinary abilities in the sciences, arts, education, business or athletics

**O-1B:** aliens of extraordinary ability in the arts or extraordinary achievement in the motion picture or television industry

**O-2:** accompanying aliens

**O-3:** spouses or children under the age of twenty-one of O-1 and O-2 visa holders

**P-1:** athletes, entertainment groups, and support personnel

**P-1A:** athletes performing individually or as part of a group or team at an internationally recognized level of performance

**P-1B:** people who perform with or are an integral or essential part of an entertainment group that has been recognized internationally as being outstanding in the specific field for a sustained and substantial period of time

**P-2:** artistic exchange (reciprocal exchange program)

**P-3:** artistic exchange (culturally unique program)

**P-4:** spouses and children under the age of twenty-one of P-1, P-2, and P-3 visa holders

**Q:** cultural exchange

**R-1:** temporary nonimmigrant religious workers

**R-2:** spouses or children under the age of twenty-one of R-1 visa holder

**S:** aliens assisting in law enforcement

**T:** victims of human trafficking

**TD:** spouses and children under the age of twenty-one of TN visa holder

**TN:** professional workers under NAFTA (for Canadians and Mexicans)

**TWOV** (transit without visa)

**U:** victims of crime

**VW:** visa waiver visitors

# APPENDIX D

# Selected Forms

**1099:** reports various types of income other than wages, salaries, and tips to the U.S. government; often used for independent contractors

**DS-160:** nonimmigrant visa application form

**DS-2019:** certificate of eligibility for exchange visitor status

**ETA-9035:** labor condition application (LCA)

**I-9:** employment eligibility verification

**I-102:** application for a new or replacement I-94 or I-95 nonimmigrant arrival-departure document

**I-129:** the basic NIV application form

**I-129F:** petition for alien fiancé(e)

**I-130:** immediate alien relative petition

**I-140:** immigrant petition for alien worker (part of the green card application process)

**I-20:** certificate for eligibility for nonimmigrant F-1 student status

**I-29:** sponsor a worker/petition to sponsor a nonimmigrant worker

**I-485:** application to register permanent residence or adjust status

**I-539:** application to extend/change nonimmigrant status

**I-765:** application for employment authorization

**I-797 form:** approval notice

**I-864:** affidavit of support form

**I-864A:** contract between sponsor and household member

**I-9 form:** employment eligibility verification

**I-94 card:** work permit; states how long you may remain legally in the United States

**I-94W card:** I-94 card for those without a visa who are entering the United States on the Visa Waiver Program

**W-2:** a form that reports an employee's annual wages and the amount of taxes withheld from his or her paycheck from the previous year

# APPENDIX E

# The NAFTA Treaty's List of Professional Jobs and Their Educational Requirements Set Forth in Appendix 1603.D.1

The four subcategories of professions are:

> General

> Medical and Allied Professionals

> Scientists

> Teachers

Within each subcategory are specific job classifications approved for TN issuance. The U.S. position being offered to the Canadian or Mexican TN visa applicant must fall under one of the job titles, and the applicant must meet the minimum qualifications listed for that occupation.

| Profession [1] | Minimum Education Requirements and Alternative Credentials |
|---|---|
| **General** | |
| Accountant | Baccalaureate or *licenciatura* degree; or C.P.A., C.A., C.G.A. or C.M.A. |
| Architect | Baccalaureate or *licenciatura* degree; or state/provincial license [2] |
| Computer systems analyst | Baccalaureate or *licenciatura* degree; or postsecondary diploma [3] or postsecondary certificate [4] and three years' experience |
| Disaster relief insurance claims adjuster (claims adjuster employed by an insurance company located in the territory of a party, or an independent claims adjuster) | Baccalaureate or *licenciatura* degree, and successful completion of training in the appropriate areas of insurance adjustment pertaining to disaster relief claims; or three years' experience in claims adjustment and successful completion of training in the appropriate areas of insurance adjustment pertaining to disaster relief claims. |
| Economist | Baccalaureate or *licenciatura* degree |
| Engineer | Baccalaureate or *licenciatura* degree; or state/provincial license |

| Profession [1] | Minimum Education Requirements and Alternative Credentials |
|---|---|
| Forester | Baccalaureate or *licenciatura* degree; or state/provincial license |
| Graphic designer | Baccalaureate or *licenciatura* degree; or postsecondary diploma or postsecondary certificate, and three years' experience |
| Hotel manager | Baccalaureate or *licenciatura* degree in hotel/restaurant management; or postsecondary diploma or postsecondary certificate in hotel/restaurant management, and three years' experience in hotel/restaurant management |
| Industrial designer | Baccalaureate or *licenciatura* degree; or postsecondary diploma or postsecondary certificate, and three years' experience |
| Interior designer | Baccalaureate or *licenciatura* degree; or postsecondary diploma or postsecondary certificate, and three years' experience |
| Land surveyor | Baccalaureate or *licenciatura* degree; or state/provincial/federal license |
| Landscape architect | Baccalaureate or *licenciatura* degree |
| Lawyer (including notary in the Province of Quebec) | LL.B., J.D., LL.L., B.C.L. or *licenciatura* degree (five years); or membership in a state/provincial bar |
| Librarian | M.L.S. or B.L.S. (for which another baccalaureate or *licenciatura* degree was a prerequisite) |
| Management consultant | Baccalaureate or *licenciatura* degree; or equivalent professional experience as established by statement or professional credential attesting to five years' experience as a management consultant, or five years' experience in a field of specialty related to the consulting agreement |
| Mathematician (including statistician) | Baccalaureate or *licenciatura* degree |
| Range manager/range conservationist | Baccalaureate or *licenciatura* degree |
| Research Assistant (working in a postsecondary educational institution) | Baccalaureate or *licenciatura* degree |
| Scientific technician/technologist [5] | Possession of (a) theoretical knowledge of any of the following disciplines: agricultural sciences, astronomy, biology, chemistry, engineering, forestry, geology, geophysics, meteorology or physics; and (b) the ability to solve practical problems in any of those disciplines, or the ability to apply principles of any of those disciplines to basic or applied research |
| Social Worker | Baccalaureate or *licenciatura* degree |
| Sylviculturist (including forestry specialist) | Baccalaureate or *licenciatura* degree |
| Technical publications writer | Baccalaureate or *licenciatura* degree; or postsecondary diploma or postsecondary certificate, and three years' experience |

| Profession [1] | Minimum Education Requirements and Alternative Credentials |
|---|---|
| Urban planner (including geographer) | Baccalaureate or *licenciatura* degree |
| Vocational counselor | Baccalaureate or *licenciatura* degree |
| **Medical/allied professional** | |
| Dentist | D.D.S., D.M.D., Doctor en Odontologia or Doctor en Cirugia Dental; or state/provincial license |
| Dietitian | Baccalaureate or *licenciatura* degree; or state/provincial license |
| Medical laboratory technologist (Canada)/medical technologist (Mexico and the United States) [6] | Baccalaureate or *licenciatura* degree; or postsecondary diploma or postsecondary certificate, and three years' experience |
| Nutritionist | Baccalaureate or *licenciatura* degree |
| Occupational therapist | Baccalaureate or *licenciatura* degree; or state/provincial license |
| Pharmacist | Baccalaureate or *licenciatura* degree; or state/provincial license |
| Physician (teaching or research only) | M.D. or Doctor en Medicina; or state/provincial license |
| Physiotherapist/Physical therapist | Baccalaureate or *licenciatura* degree; or state/provincial license |
| Psychologist | State/provincial license; or *licenciatura* degree |
| Recreational therapist | Baccalaureate or *licenciatura* degree |
| Registered nurse | State/provincial license; or *licenciatura* degree |
| Veterinarian | D.V.M., D.M.V. or *Doctor en Veterinaria*; or state/provincial license |
| **Scientist** | |
| Agriculturist (including Agronomist) | Baccalaureate or *licenciatura* degree |
| Animal breeder | Baccalaureate or *licenciatura* degree |
| Animal scientist | Baccalaureate or *licenciatura* degree |
| Apiculturist | Baccalaureate or *licenciatura* degree |
| Astronomer | Baccalaureate or *licenciatura* degree |
| Biochemist | Baccalaureate or *licenciatura* degree |
| Biologist Chemist | Baccalaureate or *licenciatura* degree |
| Dairy scientist | Baccalaureate or *licenciatura* degree |
| Entomologist | Baccalaureate or *licenciatura* degree |
| Epidemiologist | Baccalaureate or *licenciatura* degree |
| Geneticist | Baccalaureate or *licenciatura* degree |
| Geologist | Baccalaureate or *licenciatura* degree |
| Geochemist | Baccalaureate or *licenciatura* degree |

| Profession [1] | Minimum Education Requirements and Alternative Credentials |
|---|---|
| Geophysicist (including Oceanographer in Mexico and the United States) | Baccalaureate or *licenciatura* degree |
| Horticulturist | Baccalaureate or *licenciatura* degree |
| Meteorologist | Baccalaureate or *licenciatura* degree |
| Pharmacologist | Baccalaureate or *licenciatura* degree |
| Physicist (including Oceanographer in Canada) | Baccalaureate or *licenciatura* degree |
| Plant breeder | Baccalaureate or *licenciatura* degree |
| Poultry scientist | Baccalaureate or *licenciatura* degree |
| Soil scientist | Baccalaureate or *licenciatura* degree |
| Zoologist | Baccalaureate or *licenciatura* degree |
| **Teacher** | |
| College | Baccalaureate or *licenciatura* degree |
| Seminary | Baccalaureate or *licenciatura* degree |
| University | Baccalaureate or *licenciatura* degree |

[1] A business person seeking temporary entry under this appendix may also perform training functions relating to the profession, including conducting seminars.

[2] "State/provincial license" and "state/provincial/federal license" mean any document issued by a state, provincial, or federal government, as the case may be, or under its authority, but not by a local government, that permits a person to engage in a regulated activity or profession.

[3] "Postsecondary diploma" means a credential issued on completion of two or more years of postsecondary education, by an accredited academic institution in Canada or the United States.

[4] "Postsecondary certificate" means a certificate issued on completion of two or more years of postsecondary education at an academic institution, by the federal government of Mexico or a state government in Mexico, an academic institution recognized by the federal government or a state government, or an academic institution created by federal or state law.

[5] A business person in this category must be seeking temporary entry to work in direct support of professionals in agricultural sciences, astronomy, biology, chemistry, engineering, forestry, geology, geophysics, meteorology, or physics.

[6] A business person in this category must be seeking temporary entry to perform in a laboratory chemical, biological, hematological, immunologic, microscopic, or bacteriological tests and analyses for diagnosis, treatment, or prevention of disease.

Many of these jobs are clearly defined—someone is either a dentist or not, right? True. On the other hand, there is some room for interpretation on several job classifications. For example, the engineer classification may include software engineer as the engineering is not limited to one particular field. Computer systems analyst is another category with a wide berth for subjectivity.

# APPENDIX F

# Selected Internet Resources

Department of Homeland Security: http://www.dhs.gov/index.shtm

USCIS: http://www.uscis.gov/portal/site/uscis

USCIS Forms:

http://www.uscis.gov/portal/site/

# INDEX

# The Smart Guide Series

### Making Smart People Smarter

THE **SMART** GUIDE TO

## GREEN LIVING

The most complete guide to green living ever published

How green living benefits your health as well as the Earth's

How green living can save you lots of money

Why the green economy and job market is an attractive, new, lucrative frontier

Julie Kerr **Gines**

# Available Titles

Smart Guide To Astronomy
Smart Guide To Bachelorette Parties
Smart Guide To Back and Nerve Pain
Smart Guide To Biology
Smart Guide To Bridge
Smart Guide To Chemistry
Smart Guide To Classical Music
Smart Guide To Deciphering A Wine Label
Smart Guide To eBay
Smart Guide To Fighting Infections
Smart Guide To Forensic Careers
Smart Guide To Forensic Science
Smart Guide To Freshwater Fishing
Smart Guide To Getting Published
Smart Guide To Golf
Smart Guide To Green Living
Smart Guide To Healthy Grilling
Smart Guide To High School Math
Smart Guide To Hiking and Backpacking
Smart Guide To Horses and Riding
Smart Guide To Life After Divorce
Smart Guide To Making A Fortune With Infomercials
Smart Guide To Managing Stress
Smart Guide To Medical Imaging Tests
Smart Guide To Nutrition
Smart Guide To Patents
Smart Guide To Practical Math
Smart Guide To Single Malt Scotch
Smart Guide To Starting Your Own Business
Smart Guide To The Perfect Job Interview
Smart Guide To The Solar System
Smart Guide To Understanding Your Cat
Smart Guide To US Visas
Smart Guide To Wedding Weekend Events
Smart Guide To Wine

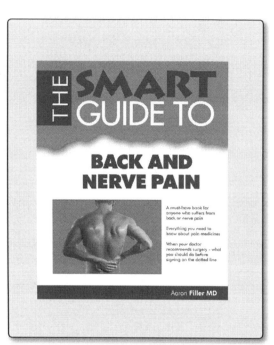

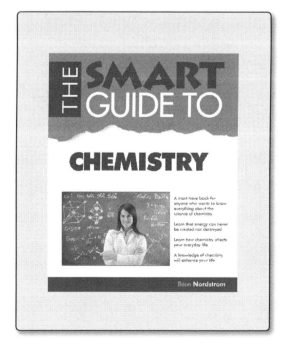

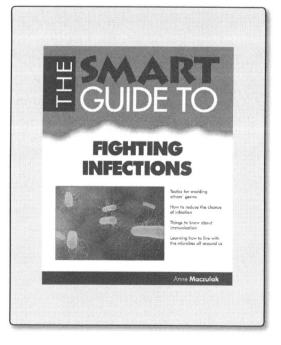

THE SMART GUIDE TO

# BIOLOGY

A must-have book for anyone who wants learn the about world of living things

Understand the workings of plant and animals

Take the first step to understanding the biosphere

Anne **Maczulak**

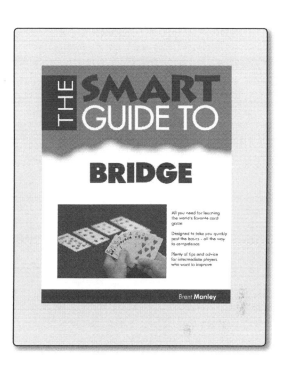

THE SMART GUIDE TO

# BRIDGE

All you need for learning the world's favorite card game

Designed to take you quickly past the basics – all the way to competence

Plenty of tips and advice for intermediate players who want to improve

Brent **Manley**

THE SMART GUIDE TO

# FORENSIC CAREERS

A must-have book for anyone who wants to a career in forensic science

How to choose a forensic science degree program

What mistakes to avoid working in forensics

How to land that first forensic job

Max **Houck**

THE SMART GUIDE TO

# FORENSIC SCIENCE

A must-have book for anyone who wants to fully understand forensic science

The science behind forensics completely explained

Learn how modern forensic sciences help solve cases

Max **Houck**

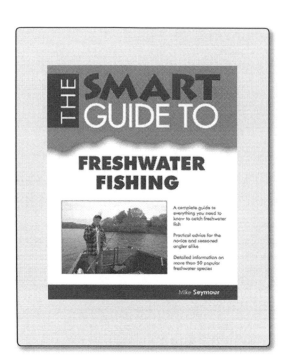

**THE SMART GUIDE TO**

## FRESHWATER FISHING

A complete guide to everything you need to know to catch freshwater fish

Practical advice for the novice and seasoned angler alike

Detailed information on more than 50 popular freshwater species

Mike **Seymour**

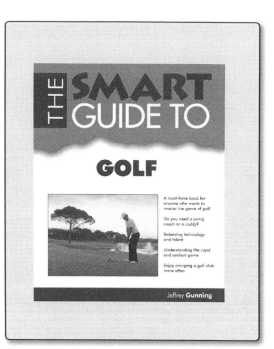

**THE SMART GUIDE TO**

## GOLF

A must-have book for anyone who wants to master the game of golf

Do you need a swing coach or a caddy?

Balancing technology and talent

Understanding the royal and ancient game

Enjoy swinging a golf club more often

Jeffrey **Gunning**

**THE SMART GUIDE TO**

## HIGH SCHOOL MATH

Know what questions your teacher is likely to ask on an exam

Study less - and get better grades

All the math you need to excel or "just get by" You decide what you need

Do as well as the nerds without having to become one

Jim **Stein**

**THE SMART GUIDE TO**

## HIKING AND BACKPACKING

A must-have book for anyone who enjoys getting into the outdoors

Useful information for both beginning and experienced hikers and backpackers

Learn how to stay safe and healthy while hiking and backpacking

Brian **Nordstrom**

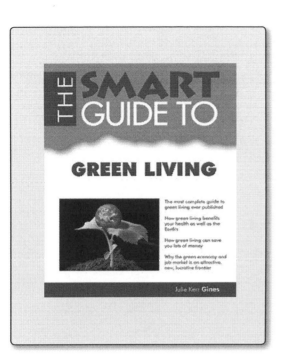

# THE SMART GUIDE TO

## GREEN LIVING

The most complete guide to green living ever published

How green living benefits your health as well as the Earth's

How green living can save you lots of money

Why the green economy and job market is an attractive, new, lucrative frontier

Julie Kerr **Gines**

# THE SMART GUIDE TO

## HEALTHY GRILLING

Low fat, low calorie grilling tips and techniques

Make succulent heart healthy burgers on your grill

Convert fish avoiders into seafood lovers

Grill fresh veggies so tasty even your kids will crave them

Barry **Fast**

# THE SMART GUIDE TO

## HORSES AND RIDING

Turn your dreams of riding a horse into reality

A complete resource for new horse owners

Communicating with and caring for horses

Skills and tips for every rider

Learn about horses, inside and out

Martha **Woodham**

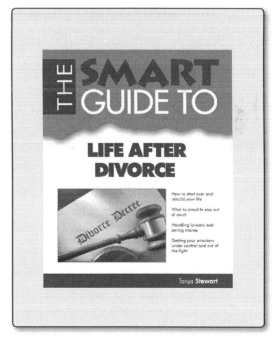

# THE SMART GUIDE TO

## LIFE AFTER DIVORCE

How to start over and rebuild your life

What to avoid to stay out of court

Handling lawyers and saving money

Getting your emotions under control and out of the fight

Tanya **Stewart**

# THE SMART GUIDE TO

## MAKING A FORTUNE WITH INFOMERCIALS

**AS SEEN ON TV.com**

How to make a powerful infomercial for only $1,000

How to pick winning products and upsells

How to write a persuasive script

Everything you need to know to make money in the infomercial industry

Kevin **Harrington**

# THE SMART GUIDE TO

## MANAGING STRESS

Tame your worries and fears

Handle unreasonable people who stress you out

Reduce tension with loved ones and co-workers

Tips to beef up your resistance to stress

Bryan **Robinson**

# THE SMART GUIDE TO

## NUTRITION

Understanding the balanced diet

Learn the truth about sugar

Learn how to spot harmful fad diets

Managing salt intake and other nutrition pitfalls

How to select nutrient-rich foods

Anne **Maczulak**

# THE SMART GUIDE TO

## PATENTS

How to protect your idea from the first moment

Getting the best possible patent on your idea

Turning a patent into a source of income

Taking the steps now so you can win big later if someone infringes

Aaron **Filler**

## THE SMART GUIDE TO
### MASTERING EBAY

A must-have book for anyone who wants to make money on eBay

Buying and selling on eBay like a pro

Building your own eBay store

Get a complete walkthrough of eBay

Nieves **Marcus**

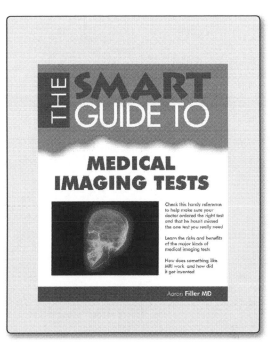

## THE SMART GUIDE TO
### MEDICAL IMAGING TESTS

Check this handy reference to help make sure your doctor ordered the right test and that he hasn't missed the one test you really need

Learn the risks and benefits of the major kinds of medical imaging tests

How does something like MRI work and how did it get invented

Aaron **Filler MD**

## THE SMART GUIDE TO
### PRACTICAL MATH

Answers to the problems you need to solve - in an easy-to-use format

Practical math problems for your home, your finances, your health, your business

Practical solutions that give you the fastest, cheapest, or easiest way to do a job

Jim **Stein**

## THE SMART GUIDE TO
### SINGLE MALT SCOTCH WHISKY

A must-have book for anyone who wants to know everything about single malt Scotch whisky

Information about all the distilleries and the whisky they make

Learn how to taste and appreciate single malt Scotch Whisky

Elizabeth Riley **Bell**

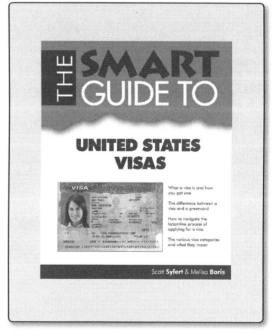

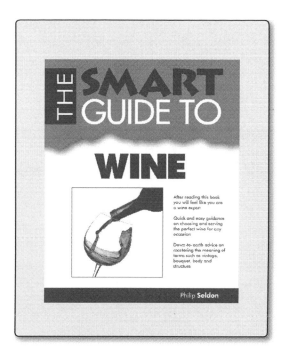

# The Smart Guide Series

Making Smart People Smarter

Smart Guides are available at your local bookseller

or from the following Internet retailers

www.SmartGuidePublications.com

www.Amazon.com

www.BarnesandNoble.com

Smart Guides are popularly priced from $18.95

Smart Guides are also available in Kindle and Nook editions

# ABOUT THE AUTHORS

## Scott Syfert

Scott Syfert is a partner with the law firm of Moore & Van Allen in Charlotte, North Carolina where he handles a variety of international transactional matters, including mergers, acquisition and other corporate restructurings, as well as their impact on U.S. visa holders.

He has over thirteen years of experience in advising clients in international and visa matters. He has written widely on a variety of international topics, including articles in leading U.S. law reviews on "U.S. Visa Options and Strategies for the Information Technology Industry," "Capitalism or Corruption? Corporate Structure, Western Investment and Commercial Crime in the Russian Federation," and "The Immigration Consequences of Mergers, Acquisitions and Other Corporate Restructuring: A Practitioner's Guide."

He is the co-founder of The Atlantic Bridge, a non-profit corporation whose purpose is to maintain the "special relationship" between the US and Great Britain.

He received a B.A. in History and Political Science (1991) and his J.D. (1997) from the University of North Carolina as well a Master's Degree in Foreign Affairs from the University of Virginia (1994), as well as studying at the London School of Economics.

## Melisa Boris

Melisa Boris is a paralegal with the law firm of Moore & Van Allen in Charlotte, North Carolina where she specializes in U.S. immigration. For over twelve years she has assisted corporate clients in a wide range of industries with nonimmigrant and immigrant visa matters. She began her career at Queens University in Charlotte where she served as a Designated School Official, advising international students on U.S. visa matters.

She received a B.S. in Communication (1992) from Ohio University and she is a North Carolina State Bar certified paralegal.